Your Dream Is Your Responsibility

Unveiling life changing principals of success for a powerful dream journey

Heaven Brown

authorHOUSE®

AuthorHouse™
1663 Liberty Drive
Bloomington, IN 47403
www.authorhouse.com
Phone: 1 (800) 839-8640

Published by AuthorHouse 10/01/2015

ISBN: 978-1-5049-4953-8 (sc)
ISBN: 978-1-5049-4952-1 (e)

Library of Congress Control Number: 2015915124

Print information available on the last page.

Contents

Introduction to dreamers

We all have dreams within the depths of our heart that we aspire to achieve. There is nothing like being in the center of your dream. We all have a dream life, and a lifestyle that we aspire to live. More often than not, we do not pursue those dreams let alone fulfill our life's purpose. If you once had a dream that you let die or you are currently pursuing your dreams and you need that extra boost of encouragement, don't worry this book is for you. If your dream has been chewed up spit out and stepped on get ready to bring back the life of your dream. You will receive that encouragement that you need to move forward towards the dream that you love so dearly. The book will teach you a different way of looking at your dream. It will also give you practical steps on how to achieve your dream as fast as possible.

One of the biggest reasons why people don't achieve their dreams is because there are obstacles standing in the way of that. One of the biggest obstacles is the question most Christians fall captive to which is: Is my dream in the will of God for my life? In the book I go into detail about how your dream fits in the plan of God. I also clarify misconceptions of whether you are to take action or just let God do it. As you pursue your dream you must understand that there are dream snatchers all around you but the biggest way that your dream can be stolen from you is through fear and distraction.

I'm going to give you various characters you know from the Holy Scripture who struggled with fear and distractions. I will also give you details about my life and how God brought me through the process of overcoming fear and distractions. If your dream is coming from a sincere place you must know that your dream is tied to your purpose somehow. I like to think of it as your dream being the daughter of your purpose. In other words your purpose in life is the bigger picture. If you can't start with fulfilling your dreams in life, how will you fulfill your purpose? If I was your enemy and I did not want you to fulfill your purpose and dream, I would simply try to distract you or make you fearful. By the end of this book you'll be able to have a clear view of your vision so that nothing can hinder you this time around.

So sit back, get a cup of tea, put your feet up and relax. You're about to receive some answers that you've been waiting on. Get ready to cast aside all of those heavy expectations that you have allowed to keep you from fulfilling your dream. As I was writing this book I was very prayerful and thankful for God giving me the words for everyone who would read this book and be moved to action. If you picked this book up it means that this title is connected to a part of you that wants to fulfill your dream, a part of you that desires to see the beauty in your life. If you are one who has nothing more than a dream, you want to start pursuing it now but don't know the first step, this book will be a blessing to you as it inspires and motivates you to run toward your dream. If you already began fulfilling your dream but for whatever reason there's a loss of enthusiasm and motivation and now you can't find a good enough reason to pick up and push through, this book is for you. It will teach you how to have a conquerors mentality so that you can bring your dream to pass faster than you ever thought possible.

The Bible is not just a theological book but you can literally transform your world through the principles of increase that are located within. Some of us can be so religious that we look at the bible as if it's only purpose it's to help us connect with God. The bible is not just a road map to Heaven; it has a goldmine of practical principals that encourage us to live our best life while we are here. In Deuteronomy 8:18 the bible says God gives us the power to get wealth, it does not say He gets the wealth for us but He gives us the power to get it. There are so many business people who stand on the principles of increase within Holy Scriptures. Many of these people are very successful entrepreneurs because they understand that there are keys to success hidden within the Scriptures. Wise people understand the key to wisdom is to pull it directly from the source when possible. If the wisest person in the world is the author of the Holy Scriptures, why not retrieve wisdom from the quickest tangible resource manual that He organized for us. This book is very insightful so get ready to go on the journey that you've been waiting for. As you read this book have an open mind about your future and where God is taking you. Enjoy!

Chapter 1

Should you pursue your dream?

Create your own world

There is a blessedness on the hands of mankind, and a gift that allows us to create our own world. Somehow, we humans have the capacity to take a portion of a rugged, nasty swamp and create it into a beautiful, refreshing, lovely park, all because we can use our imagination and dream beyond what our eyes can see.

Picture the earth and all the beauty that we experience daily, some parts are natural beauties as a result of God's imagination. Other parts of the world are shaped and landscaped from the imagination and creativity of humans. God has given us the ability to change what once was an ugly looking world after the fall, to a beautiful and comfortable home for human beings. Yes! We live in a fallen world, but it doesn't mean our imagination and dreams have to fall. I'm telling you today; if you can dream beyond your eyes, you have it within your power to create anything that you desire. God has already gifted you with the ability to shape and create your own world.

Earlier this year, God started to speak to me about creating my world. He showed me that I have the creativity within myself to create my own world. People are given opportunities because of some sort of creative gift that they have. Before a gift is discovered, it must first be uncovered; before a gift can be uncovered, it has to start with a pursuit; before it can be pursued, one has to challenge themselves to birth it out of their imagination. Some of us never pay attention to the good things that come from our imagination.

The reality is; we first came from the imagination of God Himself. He pictured us within his mind before he spoke us into existence. This is why it's hard for me to not believe that there is a God; the intricate details of our very makeup testify of God's imagination. All you have to do is look in the mirror at the beautiful person staring back at you. As you do so day by day, remember, you first began in the imagination of God himself. How awesome and wonderful it is to know that you came from the imagination of the creator of the whole universe!

Because God wanted you here, He took His imagination and spoke it into existence. Awesome right! Just like God, we have the ability to imagine our dreams and create our world. I see people who create all types of businesses, which would have never been thought of without a creative imagination; however, through the gift of imagination we have the capacity to create our world. We can even create our world with our own words. Whether you are aware of it or not, your imagination feeds your dream the food that it needs to stay creative. If you don't use your imagination, you can't have a dream; your imagination is the beginning of dreaming.

Earlier in 2014, I put a sticker above my bed that said "Dream until your dreams come true." I placed the sticker there to remind myself that no matter where I fall in this place called life, I never want to lose sight of the original dreams that were placed in my heart. Some of us are unaware of the fact that our dreams are connected to our soul; when your dream is stolen it is a sign that your soul is in jeopardy. Dreams uniquely sprout from the soul (mind, will, and emotions) of the person who imagined them. If you have a grand idea of being someone great, do not allow anyone to influence you so much that they discourage your imagination and steal your dreams entirely.

Pursuing that dream

My aim is to clarify a few things concerning whether or not a person should pursue their dream. If you are a believer, you should never set your heart out to do anything without first getting counsel from God. Reason being; God is your creator and has a predestined purpose for your life. He knows exactly what steps are necessary to get you to your blessing. For some reason, people have had a deceptive reality which suggests that God is the sole steward of our dream.

Often, this becomes a setback for upcoming dreamers. If you are one who has a dream, the first thing a religious person will tell you is that you don't need to get ahead of God, just wait on His timing, and He will bring it to pass for you. This advice is partially true; the problem I have with this statement is that the person who is giving the advice has usually not consulted God for their own dreams. Their assuming God expects you to do nothing but pray. Most people generally don't know how to pray, let alone hear from God. If you tell them they need to hear from God prior to starting their dream; you should tell them exactly how to do so, or else they will be waiting forever. This is unacceptable for a person who desires to see their dream come to pass. I believe there has to be a balance between waiting on God and putting your dream to work.

God speaks to us in various ways. Your confirmation is not always going to come to your spirit; however, it can come through a sign or by someone else's words. We need to make sure that our spirit is in tune with Him so that we can pick up on his direction. Surely, He will give you signs along the way that help guide your path; whether you should go left or right.

Proverbs 3:6

"In all your ways acknowledge Him, and He shall direct your path."

How awesome is it, when you experience God confirming everything that you have set your heart out to do, directing your path every step of the way? When you have an overwhelming desire to start your dream, it's usually because He has sewn a seed in your heart.

Your Dream is Your Responsibility

If God has given you ideas, inventions, businesses or ministries, then they are your responsibility. Sitting around waiting on someone to give you an opportunity is not how God expects you to pursue your dream. You cannot be timid about your Dream. People who are timid usually have a mentality that says "If it's meant to be for me, it will happen." In my opinion, this is a peasant mentality. The only way peasants receive is when someone else gives to them. Keep in mind; if you never pursue it, it will never happen.

I've noticed that God has given me ideas in the past; instead of doing the legwork, I thought of every excuse as to why I shouldn't pursue it. If there is a ministry that God has given you, you mustn't be afraid to pursue it. After all God has an appointed time for every dream. He gave it to you today instead of yesterday because today is the appointed time for you to start pursuing it.

In 2013, I started getting speaking engagements, people were contacting me out of the blue. God expressed to me that he had already released me to go forward, but I kept thinking it wasn't necessary to stay connected, because God will do it for me. This mindset kept me enslaved to believing that God doesn't want me to lift a finger.

We have it on the inside of us to make our lives whatever we desire. No one is stopping us, if it isn't happening it's only because we are getting in our own way. My friend and I went to a festival once, after we paid our way at the door we began to walk down the aisle of the festival. It had vendor shops and food stands on both sides, but the aisle was short-lived and only stretched for about one-fourth of a mile. It was very disappointing because we were under the impression that it was a huge festival. We thought we would meet more vendors, authors, business owners, and even have more food options.

We got to the end and there was a guy who had a T-shirt stand, he was waiting on us to come to his stand, but he saw that we were not interested so he decided to get up and come to us. He spoke negative words about the festival. He said, "Do you see how much these people think of you? They couldn't even give you more options for the festival." He suggested that we should be offended because the festival was a real rip-off. I walked away because he started to use profanity, plus his approach was too negative. I realized that this man is the only person in his own way; he developed the concept for why he was oppressed.

At some point we have to take responsibility for our own lives. We all have an equal opportunity to make our dream a reality. All of us have it within our power to make our own lives beautiful; in America we all have freedom and liberty to make our dreams come to past. His oppression was deeply rooted from his mentality and his views on life. Even after experiencing racism first-hand, I am convinced that I'm in control of the outcome of my life and my purpose. There are many influences, but you are the executive decision maker in your world! Be encouraged and know that your life changes when you change your mindset.

The Mouse Test

Everything happens in God's timing, so whether you pursue your dreams today or tomorrow, He will still bring it to pass in His own time, but you are still required to pursue it.

Proverbs 16:9

Says "*A man's heart plans his way but the Lord directs his steps.*"

Can He not do it? Is He not God? Some people are afraid to step out on faith because they fear that they are moving too quickly, we forget that God works in eternity and has the ability to recover us from any mishap or mistake. Sometimes we forget that He is all knowing.

It's just like if you had a pet mouse and you placed him inside of a maze. You put the cheese at the finish line, the cheese represents his dream that he has been waiting on all his life. You, being his superior, have the ability to see his progress from a birds-eye view. You can see every move he makes even if he makes no moves at all. He cannot think like you neither can he understand your words because he's a mouse. So you position yourself to help him along his journey of finding his dream cheese.

You see that he is heading in the wrong direction, so you place a stumbling block in his path to prevent him from going too far off course. Not to mention the voices he hears of the other mice in the room making fun of him. Often, when he gets discouraged he looks up at you with his sad, discouraging eyes and somehow communicates to you that he needs your help; you then reach out and place a crumb near the path that you want him to go so that he can get closer to his dream cheese.

Throughout this time, he can smell the cheese and he becomes encouraged. Just when he feels like he's getting somewhere, here comes another stumbling block. He doesn't understand that hitting a dead end is just a sign that he needs to go in a different direction. The dead end is not to discourage him but rather to protect him.

So he moves along and eventually catches on to the structure and patterns of the maze, so much that he can even predict if the next turn will lead him into a brick wall. This insight gives him the ability to speed up on his journey. Instead of going at a slow pace, he is now able to increase his speed. He eventually gets to his cheese and takes it to an area where all the other mice can see.

You'd think that this little mouse is going to hog all the cheese and not share a crumb, but instead, he gives a little bit to each of the other mice and shares with them the secrets of how to get through the maze. In case you didn't catch on, the mouse represents us, the person represents God, the other mice represent people who discourage you, the cheese represents your dream that you are after and the maze represents the process needed to get you to your dream.

Here's what I'm trying to convey to you. Even though your dream is your responsibility, if you pursue your dreams, God has a way of making all things work together for your own good, because you love Him and are called according to His purpose. Your concern should never be whether or not you should pursue your dream. If you never budge, you give God nothing to work with.

Pay close attention to the relationship between the mouse and the person. If the mouse would've been too fearful to go after that cheese, there would've been no way for the person to help him get there. If you want to see your dreams come to pass it is very important that you get up and make it happen. You cannot leave God to do everything for you.

> **James 2:17 *says "thus also faith by itself, if it does not have works, is dead."***

I would rather use others

The way a person can view money as an opportunity to come up, is the same way a person can view other people as an opportunity to come up. These types of people view everyone who comes into their life as nothing more than money to be spent. Their mindset is usually 'how can I use this person to the best of my ability?' If you're a part of their life, they will eventually suck you dry. Whenever you offer to help, they will usually end up begging for more as if you are obligated. God forbid you don't help them out; the next trick they try is the guilt trip.

These are the type of people that cast their respon-sibilities on others. They always blamed others for why they are unable to do things for themselves. This type of person is someone who'd rather other people bring their dream on a silver platter. If we truly want to see our dream meet our future we cannot depend on or use others along the way. If someone isn't helping you with your dream, please don't take it personal just know that your dream is your responsibility.

If this has been your mentality, I want to release you from the ignorance of believing that you can be lazy and your dreams will still happen for you. For some people it happens immediately because they just so happen to be in the right place at the right time, but for others it are not so easy. If you want to eat, you have to go after your meal. I noticed that God will give us resources, but He will not cheat for us. The resources are to equip you to pass the class, but if you never get out of the bed to go and take that test, you would never pass. Please! Whatever you do, don't allow yourself to think with a lazy mentality. God will not do the work for you, He will help you along the way as you seek His counsel, but it is up to you to execute your dream.

Use your imagination

The first thing that God allowed Adam to do was to use his imagination in:

Genesis 2:19-20

"Out of the ground the Lord God formed every beast of the field and every bird of the air, and brought them to Adam to see what he would call them. And whatever Adam called each living creature that was its name, so Adam gave names to all the cattle, to the birds of the air, and to every beast of the field."

It says that God brought the animals to Adam. This lets us know that God will bring opportunities to us in order to stimulate our imagination. He brings Adam a woman to see what his imagination will call her. Because she resembled Adam and had the same bone structure and flesh as he, his imagination said that her name is 'woman'. The reality is that this creature being taken out of man was already considered to be a woman. So God bringing her to Adam was to give him the opportunity to align his thoughts and imagination with God's.

We often look at the Scripture and we see that God brought the woman to Adam, but we tend to skip over the part where it says that God brought the animals to Adam. It's very important that we grasp this part because some people think that it was Adams job to name the animals. But Adam's job was not to name the animals. Adam's job was to till the ground. Naming the animals was God's way of getting Adam to use his imagination, which is the same way school teaches students to use their imagination to understand concepts.

I encourage everyone I see to think outside of the box and get creative with their imagination and their thoughts. The thing about creative imagination is that you cannot go wrong. Something may be a bit far-fetched from your budget, but all things are possible. Now we know that even the moon is reachable because mankind used their imagination to get there. Be fearful for what? Sir Winston Churchill said "Success is the ability to go from failure to failure, without a loss of enthusiasm."

Many of us have the zeal to start a business and to pursue our dreams. I have an aunt who has had a desire to finish cosmetology school. Every so often something would happen where she was unable to finish school and make that dream a reality. But one day she finished school and the one thing no one could deny, was that she never lost her zeal or enthusiasm to see her dream come to pass.

If you are one who has failed a few times to the point that people have laughed at you, I'm telling you to rejoice and be happy because you my friend, are on the path of success! Do not let the fear of failure and what others think ruin your imagination or your dream.

You are worth your dream

Self-worth issues are usually rooted from some sort of mental abuse, received from others in the past. The weird thing about self-worth is that it is a borrowed inaccurate depiction of you. If you have borrowed someone else's opinion or views of yourself, you must give it back before stepping foot toward your dream. You will need to reconsider the lies that you believed in the past about you and your inabilities. Understand that God turns impossibility into ability. We are often very harsh on ourselves when it comes to doing anything.

For whatever reason, some people are afraid to go forward. In some cases, it's because of the unknown. In other cases, it's a lack of confidence. Believe it or not, there are a lot of people who struggle with self-worth, which is why getting started on their dream seems so far away to them. Before you step into your dream, you must know that you are already worth your dream. Yes, you can have it and yes you're really worth it. We are usually too concerned with what everyone else thinks.

Some of us don't want to make moves because we're afraid that people will think we are trying to be important. If you go into a dream, understand that people are going to think whatever they want, but it has nothing to do with you or the dream inside of you. Some people have self-worth issues and they go to the extreme and become over flashy and unrealistic in their image. They start to buy expensive cars to show off. Everything they do is to prove to others their self-worth.

Then you have some who go the opposite way. These individuals actually know their self-worth and genuinely desire to express it, but because of the fear of what other people will say they take the lowly road and become frustrated in their contentment. They continually express a look that says 'Woe is me.' People who find themselves in these circumstances are so focused on what others think of them, that they never fulfill their own purpose.

Chapter 2

What is my Purpose?

Self-Awareness

Before you start each day you should genuinely dedicate yourself to being self-aware and maintaining a sense of peace within. Pursuing that peace with God every morning will ignite a more centered confident peace with yourself and others you encounter. Keeping in mind that you have a purpose and your life is worth something bigger that people can see will motivate you to stay joyful and happy. When life starts to get us down we naturally revert to thoughts of our purpose and begin asking ourselves why are we here in the first place and if we can't see anything good even in our prerifrial view, some of us start thinking of suicide and a way to end the agony of being purposeless. This is why keeping a centered sense of self-awareness can lead to a more positive outlook on life.

Your purpose and your call are intertwined; there is no way that you can understand every aspect of it through just a simple conversation. Your purpose is always unfolding as you go on in life. You will discover that various things had to happen in order to get you to where you are right now. Sometimes life can seem so purposeless, especially when you have nothing to look forward to. I believe everyone deserves to breathe the weightless air that this world offers, and to experience the beauty of living a wonderful life. Some of us rarely sit back and enjoy the things that are in front of us. I guarantee you, if we did that more often we would have more revelation about the beauty of life. Most of us live our lives the best way we know how, some of us are taught to live our lives like our parents and grandparents. Others are taught by peers and mentors.

How many of us actually take the time to imagine our lives being complete and whole? I believe our lives will begin to fill up with entirety when we start to fulfill our dreams. Every time you achieve a dream you allow more sunshine to enter your life. There is a light that we are all called to walk in, it is the light of our purpose that God predestined for us. Each day that our purpose begins to unfold, we will start to see ourselves as living the good life.

Calculated Days

After the flood in Noah's day, the Lord reduced our lifespan significantly. if we were to go by the Gregorian international calendar, also known as the 'Western calendar' consisting of dates based on time. This calendar was adopted and introduced in February 1582 by Pope Gregory XIII. I will be using this calendar as an analogy to help us calculate our days.

To begin with, our lifespan was between 800-900 years, after the flood God reduced them significantly to around 120 years. When you do the calculations and divide those years into a number of days, it is interesting to know that those who were to live for 900 years lived for around 300,000 days in total. For those who lived 120 years, had approximately 40,000 days. But now, the average life expectancy of the Human is 90 years maximum, and the lifespan of a 90 year old is, approximately 30,000 days.

Let's just say you sat down with God and He explained to you exactly how those days may be spent. The first 10,000 would consist of growing up and getting an education. Another 8000 would be dedicated to raising children and trying to figure out what your purpose is. 5000 spent working and maintaining business. 5000 spent pursuing your dreams. 2000 spent fulfilling the call on your life. Though some of these years are overlapping, this is a hypothetical analogy for the purpose of getting you to understand that we can decide exactly how these days should be spent.

The wonderful thing about God is that He already knows how many days are assigned to you. He has the capacity to lead you in the most beneficial way so that you can get the best out of your life. This is why we need God's input on fulfilling our purpose. There is no reason why we should have the right to know how all of our days will play out. If we did, there would be no reason to have a continual relationship with the Lord.

God's Omniscience

For some reason, we believe that it is God who chooses how our days will be spent, but this is simply not true. Man has free will to do what we please with our days, and to plan according to how we see fit. God is omniscient, meaning He is all-knowing. If God is all-knowing, that means He is fully aware of how we spend our days. God is past tense, present tense, future tense. He knew how we spent our days in the past, He knows how we spend our days currently and He knows how we will spend our days in the future. Why not allow God to order our days and direct our footsteps, especially if He already knows what is going to happen.

Many of us send prayers that suggest that God does not know what is going on in our lives. Our purpose is continually unfolding before the face of God. This Scripture in Jeremiah explains it well:

Jeremiah 1:5

"Before I formed you in the womb I knew you, before you were born I set you apart; I appointed you as a prophet to the nations."

Also, Chuck D. Pierce wrote in his book '*God's unfolding battle plan*':

"As our maker, God designed us intentionally with a body clock. He knows our most productive times. More importantly, he knows the best time for us to seek him, and he knows how to get us in his perfect timing. But unfortunately, when humanity sinned in the garden and brought the fall, it affected more than just our spiritual alignment with the father."

Our Flesh is Weak

Our flesh is very weak at times, and it can be very difficult to pray. Talking to God is not the easiest thing to do when you are hungry, sleepy or if you don't have a clear mind. If you want your days to be ordered by the Lord, there is going to come a time when you will need to arrest your flesh.

Galatians 5:17

"For the flesh lusts against the Spirit, and the spirit against the flesh: these are contrary to the other: so that you cannot do the things that you wish.

Chuck D. Pierce also explained in his book *'God's unfolding battle plan'*:

"Our bodies were thrown a screw as well. Now we find a body that reads these changes and an internal clock that struggles to control us. We must be willing to allow God to order our time so that we can seek him. Jesus displayed this principle when dealing with his disciples during a crucial time in his life."

Matthew 26:40 – 41

"Then He came to the disciples and found them sleeping, and said to Peter, 'what! Could you not watch with me one hour? Watch and pray, lest you enter into temptation. The spirit indeed is willing but the flesh is weak.'"

The flesh will not submit without a challenge, this means, every day we should render some sort of sacrifice to God that makes our flesh uncomfortable. This is necessary if we want to hear from the Lord regarding our purpose and our dream.

Your Purpose is not married to just one thing

As we saw in the analogy of the complete purpose for one person's life, you can see how boring it appears when calculated by numbers. When I began to understand that my days were numbered, I realized that I am here for various reasons. I understand that my purpose is a daily walk through life. For example your purpose is bigger than one thing. Your purpose consists of childbearing, being a doctor, being a motivational speaker or becoming a lawyer. You are purposed for all of these things and you are not limited to just one of them. God has created you to hold many titles such as an Author, CEO, Pastor, Doctor, Judge, Father, Sister, and so on and so forth. In other words, your purpose is literally whatever God suggests for you that day.

This should sum up the question that everyone has. 'Why am I here?' So many of us have become frustrated because we know we have an alternate purpose in life, but the frustration comes in because we are confusing it with a dream. Remember, your dream is the daughter of your purpose, and your purpose is the mother of your dream. We know that a mother can have as many children as she desires to complete her family. This is the same with us; we can have as many dreams as we want to complete our purpose. As your purpose unfolds daily, you will start to see that you were not placed here on this earth just to do one particular thing. Your purpose is complete when you have fulfilled your dreams along with the call of God for your life.

I've had people ask me about the call of God on their lives and how they should pursue it. There are some misconceptions about our purpose versus our call. The call of God is a broad statement as well as your life's purpose. The call of God has many different facets attached to it. When I turned 20, the Lord started to reveal to me, the call that was on my life. What I assumed was that this call to ministry was my purpose. What I did not understand was that it was not my complete purpose, but merely a part of it. I now know that God's purpose for my life is to have a family, speak into the lives of others, direct people to the Lord Jesus Christ and own businesses. Furthermore, I know that this is just a portion of my purpose in life.

Remember, your call is not your purpose and your purpose is not your call. If you have a call on your life, do not limit yourself to just that call. If you have a dream that you have envisioned for years, do not limit yourself to just that dream. God desires for us to have an open mind when it comes to our future, simply because he lives through us. When we limit ourselves, we are literally limiting God from being able to move in this earth realm through us. Keep in mind that God does not do it for us, but rather through us.

I was so happy when I got this revelation, because for a while, I was trained to believe that I was limited to becoming just one thing in life. Back in school, whenever a new class would start, the teacher would ask the students to introduce themselves and to tell the class what they would like to be when they grow up. Many of the students would shout out answers that they thought were cool and some would be more specific by saying a lawyer, doctor, pilot, nurse or teacher. All of these answers were great, but notice that we were only encouraged to say one thing. I went through life assuming that I could only be one thing, but in my mind, I took it differently then the way the question was intended. Believe it or not, as simple and innocent as the question appears to a child, it is the very question that shapes the way they see their lives.

The teacher was not asking the question to limit me, but rather to get me to open my mind to the possibility of greatness. Even though I forgot half of the answers that I gave, somehow I still believe that I was only destined to be one thing in life. Growing up, I searched for my purpose. I was trained that I am only suitable to be one thing. I understand the concept of having a degree consisting of a couple of different concentrations, but because society believes that if you master one thing really well, you will get the maximum amount of return on your investment.

Although I believe there are some truths to this concept, I also believe that it can be accidentally interpreted in the wrong way, a way that limits people. The truth is a person is more respected when they can say they've been a nurse for 18 years. But it is even more exciting to see this person walking into their complete purpose that they were supposed to fulfill. I'm only suggesting that you do not limit yourself by thinking you are only purposed for one thing.

You are dealing with a God who has a big claim for your life. Not only would you be doing yourself a disservice, but God as well. Dream big, when you begin to fulfill your complete purpose, you give God the opportunity to enjoy you at your best, by doing what you are purposed to.

The reason why this is so important is because I see so many people in jobs and careers that they really hate. They are unfulfilled and discouraged, after spending four years getting a degree that they come to realize they never really wanted to begin with. They also have the added pressure of paying off their student loans. The main reason people choose the careers that they have, is usually due to the financial benefits that will significantly cover their household expenses. In reality, most people would rather stay home and do nothing, than to punch the clock for the career that they cannot stand.

It's so sad to see people in this situation, people who want so much more out of life, but instead, they settle and eventually forget about the dream that they once had. Maybe it requires too much time, money and energy to start something new. I want to encourage you that it is never too late for you to fulfill your dream. You are not dead, so there is no reason why you cannot get started. Forget about the impossibilities that will come to discourage you and make you feel as though it can never happen. God specializes in things that are impossible and God can do what no other power can do. The older you get, the more odds you will have against you, which means you will have more obstacles to overcome. This is why you cannot wait another day! Your dream belongs to you! It is your responsibility to get up and redeem it! If there are any resources that you are in need of, let your request be made known to God and He will be faithful to give you whatever is required for that dream.

Chapter 3

Let's Start with Fear

Just like God made His dream a reality, we must also do the same. His dream was His responsibility and so is yours. Fear and distraction, are probably the two main reasons for why you haven't fulfilled your dream. These are common obstacles that can be overcome at any time. If you are someone who believes in your dream enough to overcome these obstacles, then you will definitely get there. Your will has to be stronger than your desire Both are direct and indirect devices used against you to get you as far away from your dream as possible. Fear encourages us to lose all faith, not only in God, but in our dreams too. When we experience fear we get distracted with various obstacles in order to completely throw us off course, so that we are unable to fulfill our purpose.

Your Mind's Battlefield

Every battle that you have, willed first began in your mind before it manifests. Sometimes we believe that other people are our enemies, when in reality we are usually our own worst enemy. Some of us don't even have to worry about the devil fighting us, because we are so good at doing his job for him. For this reason when we purposely include God in our plans, He will help us to overcome these problems. Chuck Pierce gives us so many keys on how we can win against the wars of our mind. By including God in our mindset, we will be amazed with the way things unfold for us.

It's All a Trick

Our dream is always on the line. We must understand that the enemy's desire is to directly and indirectly steal our dreams. Directly, he tries to steal it with fear. Indirectly, he tries to purchase it with distractions. I am going to open your eyes to the trickery that is against your dream. Your dream holds much value, which is why it should cost you everything. Your dream in its entirety represents one complete work, which carries the capacity to be a blessing to so many people.

If I were an enemy sent out to destroy you, the first thing I would come for is your dream. If I stop your dreams from coming to pass, that gives me the opportunity to hinder the dreams of the people directly connected to you, such as your family and friends. Some of you may not understand how much of a big deal this is, but keep reading because God is not only going to enlighten your understanding about yourself, He is going to expose you to some tricks of the enemy, starting with fear.

Fear is something that is not usually brought up in everyday conversation. No one wants to admit that the real reason they are not pursuing their dream is because they're fearful. We always have a crutch and an excuse for why things are not working out. Most of us are afraid of failing and looking bad. Fear creeps in and says: "It will never happen for you; you know you can't do this; no one is on your side." The spirit of fear, will make you feel as though nobody cares, it will even have you believing that God exists and that He loves you, but that He will never bless you. The Bible lets us know fear is a spirit and God did not give it to us.

> **2ⁿᵈ Tim 1:7 *"For God has not given us the spirit of fear; but of power, and of love, and of a sound mind."***

Fear of the Lord

Not all fear is bad, the Bible tells us:

> **Ecclesiastes 12:13 *"Let us hear the conclusion of the whole matter: Fear God and keep His commandment, for this is the duty of all mankind."***

This type of fear keeps us in line with the word and with a reverence toward God. Job was a man who feared God. I believe this is one of the reasons why the Lord was so intrigued and impressed with Job's reverence and fear for Him. We can clearly see that his challenges were simply because of his fear of the Lord. When you're a strong individual, sometimes God will allow you to be tested in areas He already knows you will pass. The Bible tells us how Job went early in the morning to sacrifice burnt offerings for his children, just in case they sinned against God and cursed God in their hearts. It tells us that this was his regular custom and that he was afraid of offending God. So this type of fear should be in the heart of every believer. The Bible tells us in:

Psalm 34:7 *"The angel of the Lord encamps around those who fear Him, and delivers them."*

Fearing God has great benefits and comes with the angel of the Lord. I think about when I first got saved, if I did something wrong, I felt the reverence and fear of God immediately. It wasn't necessarily people whom I feared, but rather a fear of disappointing God. I was living from a works mentality, but you can never go wrong when you fear the Lord. Pursuing your dream in the fear of the Lord will enhance your sensitivity to God's leading throughout the process.

General Fear

This type of fear is common amongst most of us looking to pursue anything in life. Fear is the enemy embarking on the territory of our minds with a desire to steal, kill and destroy every good thing that exists. Fear is a spirit that creates a stronghold in our mind so that we cannot move forward in life.

General Fear is not always detected and usually goes under the radar because it is the norm and has been there so long. Some of us have business ideas and dreams of becoming someone great. We know the proper steps to achieving these goals for ourselves, but because of general fear we refuse to go forward. Some of us have a fear of what people think or how they will look at us.

For some reason in today's society, people are afraid of others superseding them and being more successful in their endeavors. Subconsciously knowing this, we never want to be looked at like we're trying to outdo or be better than our peers. People have a habit of hating on dreamers. Joseph had a dream that his friends and family just couldn't understand, and because they couldn't comprehend what God was doing, their first reaction was to hate on his dream.

Some of us fear that it's not the right time, or that we don't have all of the resources that we need. These things may be true but it's no excuse to fear. All you need to do is prayerfully position yourself for preparation, so that when the time comes you are ready for take-off. The 'little ole me' mentality has to stop, because if God will do it for one He will do it for another. The bible says:

Romans 2:11 "For there is no partiality with God"

If you have a dream or a vision that God is giving you, the Lord is instructing me to tell you to have no fear, pursue your dream and He will bring it to pass.

Tormenting Fear

Tormenting fear is the type of fear that keeps you captive, only because you are not aware of how to be free. This type of fear will have you saying things that you know others want to hear, because you're afraid that they will disagree with anything that comes from your mouth. This comes with a lot of distress as it feeds on your self-esteem.

Usually with tormenting fear, something horrible has happened in the past that causes you to feel like you're a slave. Take Genesis 32:7 for example where Jacob stole his brother's birthright, because of this he was constantly running and being tormented in his mind. He was under the assumption that his brother was going to kill him for what he had done. What Jacob did not understand, was that he was being led by fear. One day he decided to face that fear and Instead of running he agreed to be in his brother's presence. He decided it didn't matter if he lived or died, but that he was not running anymore.

Just like Jacob, we have to come to a place where we decide that we will no longer run from our past. We have to be courageous, and face it this is the only way through. It doesn't matter how much you've done wrong in your past, if you want to move forward into your future, you must first make things right with anything that could possibly come to haunt you. I'm pretty sure Jacob was ashamed for what he did, by having his wives, kids, servants and employees along with him; they too, became exposed to the truth about him being a schemer. Not only does he have to be honest with himself and the people around him, but he has to face the biggest mistake of his life.

Some of us have made mistakes in our pasts that we are not proud of; maybe it has been a mistake toward someone very close to us. This is where we ought to have no shame. I will get more into that in the next section. Living in fear and beating yourself up about your past is like slowly committing spiritual suicide. God does not want us committing suicide; neither does he want us tormented by our past. He forgave you and now your slate is wiped clean. He wants you to pick up the pieces and move forward. As you do this, He will surely restore everything that you've lost in the past.

File Bankruptcy on Fear

This type of fear will have you fortify yourself so that no one can find you and remind you of anything that happened in your past. This type of fear will cause you to isolate yourself, because you don't want anyone to hurt you again. It will have you worried, confused and ashamed. Worry is the daughter of fear. One way in which we can tell that someone has had fear on their mind, is when they become worried. The effects of fear usually produce worry, neither are of God, they are two spirits that come from the enemy to make you believe that your life is over.

I know sometimes, you feel you're paying on the inside for what you have done, or for what someone else has done to you, but it doesn't mean you have to go broke over it. By saying this, I mean that fear has its effects on the human body, which can trigger stress levels to go up causing high blood pressure. Nerve damage is also caused through worrying too much. If this is you can you see that holding on to fear is costing you more than you can afford to pay? I know someone is reading this and saying, "But Heaven, you don't know what I've been through, it's bad and I don't know how to recover." Well my friend, I will tell you this, if it is that bad, then you need to file bankruptcy on that situation.

When I say file bankruptcy I mean, first accept how this situation has affected your life and if it has gotten so out of your control, then there is probably not much you can do to change it. However, you can let it go. Bankruptcy allows you to say "Yes my situation has become so bad to the point that I need a new start, so I'm taking my life and I'm starting afresh, no more fear, no more shame, no more worry and no regrets." This declaration will empower you to walk in your purpose without guilt and shame, following you everywhere you go.

God is Your Protector

One of my favorite scriptures is in Psalm and it says:

Psalms 27:1 "The Lord is my light and my salvation of whom shall I fear? The Lord is the strength of my life; of whom shall I be afraid?"

Honestly, when the Lord has your heart and you get so caught up in God, there is truly nothing or no one that you should be afraid of. It's almost like you have a humongous bodyguard who's grand in stature and protective in nature. This bodyguard has an assignment and a duty to protect you no matter what. Imagine if you have four of them around you at all times. They are always with you, keeping watch over your safety. Wouldn't this alone make you feel secure? This is how protected we should feel, especially when we know that God is on our side.

The Box Doesn't Fit

Most of the shame that people experience usually has to do with their lack of confidence. Some of us are afraid to be ourselves, because it costs us everything.

This should never be a compromise, simply because all women, men, boys and girls have something unique and particular to offer to this world. If this was not the case, God would have surely made us all the same. We are all gifts wrapped in different ways with different colors, shapes and sizes.

One thing that I noticed about myself is that when I was younger, I dealt with a lot of insecurities, mainly because of other kids teasing me. Every child needs someone to protect their emotions, and because I didn't have this emotional protection growing up, I looked for it in other people particularly men. Somehow I knew I was unique and different, but I also thought I was weird and crazy. I was teased and called names that really hurt by my friends and peers, but because I wanted to be strong, I never allowed anyone to know how hurt I was.

I knew I didn't fit into the box that people wanted for me, so I made a conscious decision to protect myself at all costs. The person that I became was a defensive, strong, independent, overbearing and protective woman. Without having a mother and a father in my life, I naturally jumped into those roles.

This was not always a good thing. I looked up one day and found that it was hard for me to be vulnerable to anyone. People thought I was very harsh and mean. I even had a woman refer to me as being too controlling. I believe Gods desire for His woman is to be vulnerable and strong without being overbearing and controlling. After reading a book called 'Captivating' by John and Staci Eldredge, I understood the true role of a woman. This book helped me to understand that it's okay to be as soft, loving and gentle as I want. I believe this book is for every female out there because it helps us to understand the true heart of a woman, including things that we don't know about ourselves.

Where is the Real Me

During my childhood, I remember times when I showed people the real me; I revealed my true thoughts, attitude and personality as a whole. However, somewhere after I turned 20, I looked up and realized that I had lost touch with my true self. I was in a crisis because it had been missing for years. Now, I have become so unidentifiable, I don't know when I lost myself or even how to get back to being that person. I'm allowing people to crush my heart all because I don't know who or where the real me is. When a person loses touch with who they are, they're usually at their most vulnerable state, because they often cling on to the first person that comes along and offers them a sense of belonging. This is when you find people in abusive relationships, drugs and gangs.

Searching For Myself

Even as a new Christian I knew Christ before I knew myself, which was the best thing that could ever happen to me. Sometimes when people find themselves before they have Christ they have a tendency to be proud, boastful, and arrogant. When a person gets to know Jesus, they no longer search to find themselves; they understand that the search is now for their identity in Christ.

There was this elderly woman who I called Mama, she lived at the nursing home that I used to work at back in 2009. Before she passed we were walking down the hallway singing hymns together, as we finished she looked at me and said "Baby! God is going to show you who you are and whose you are." I felt like the disciples when Jesus was giving them various parables, I just didn't understand what she meant. Even until this day, that particular saying is unfolding within my mind. I did not know who I was because if I did, I would not have made the reoccurring mistakes of trying to be someone else over the years. I also did not know whose I was; if I did I would not have tried to belong as much.

There's Only One Me

For some reason I grew up thinking that the person that I am is not accepted in this world. Naturally, I took on the personalities of the people around me, not understanding that there is only one me that this world has to offer. No one told me that it was okay to be myself, so I hid behind goofiness to cover up the real me. I felt as if everything I liked or the way I would express myself was not commonly acceptable. The box that I lived in made me ashamed and uncomfortable whenever I would step out and be me. I was always undecided about everything, feeling like I needed the opinions or approval of others. Most people don't know that this is something called rejection, that victimizes people especially people of creativity.

If you are one who is dealing with an identity crisis in this world, know that you are the only one who can be you. There's only one person who thinks exactly like you think, who talks exactly like you talk, and who can do exactly what you can do.

I think it's so sad when I see people trying to be like everyone else, it all boils down to one simple thing. Everyone is fearful of being themselves, for some reason, none of us like the person that we really are. Understand that if you are going to follow your dreams, you have to be okay with being yourself at all times, even if the environment suggests that you need to act like someone else. When we choose to take on another personality, not only are we stealing identities that don't belong to us, but we are also offending God. This behavior suggests that He made a mistake when He created you.

If we want to go forward in our dream with full confidence, we must be satisfied with the person that God created us to be. You must be okay with how you're built, your voice, your ideas and your personality as a whole. I don't see anything wrong with making minor changes to enhance these areas for the good, but to completely transform yourself into another person is to suggest that the original work of God was a mistake. Whatever you do, never fear being yourself. Keep in mind that people receive you best when you are who you're created to be.

Chapter 4

Fear of Rejection

In the process of pursuing your dream, it's likely that you will develop a fear of being rejected, weather it's from a test or from people rejecting you, but it is so important that you don't allow this to get in the way. When I started to fulfill my dream, I was required to step out from my comfort zone and connect with new people; this was so that I could let other business owners know who I was and what I had to offer. If I would have allowed the fear of getting rejected by the people I needed to connect with take over, I would not have fulfilled the important steps toward my dream. By becoming so fearful that it stops you from pursuing your dream, you are literally hindering a part of your purpose in life.

My friend Stacy and I were sitting out at a pool one day; her niece and another young girl were swimming at separate ends of the pool. Both little girls were around the age of 11. They were very anti-social, and did not attempt to play with each other. We figured that they were distant because they were unfamiliar with one another. A few minutes later another young girl, 4 year old Catlin came along and jumped in the pool with them. This little girl was so full of life and had a big personality; she started to play and socialize with both girls. When we looked up again they were all laughing and playing freeze tag together.

As we observed their interaction, we discovered that Caitlin's ability to get the other two girls to play together was because of her lack of fear. With them being older, they had already faced rejection and fear of acceptance to some capacity. When we are very young, our innocent minds tell us that anyone can be a friend. We have no reservations in expressing our true feelings, but as we get older, we often experience hurt and rejection, which cause us to be more comfortable with keeping ourselves reserved. At some point, in order to move past the fear of not being accepted, we must acknowledge that rejection will come regardless, but it doesn't have to hinder our dreams.

Small Man, Big World

Some of us have that small man big world mentality; we look at everything and everyone as though they are higher and more qualified than us. I want to encourage you to realize; if God gave you a dream, He has already made you good enough for it. As you go through and complete the progressive qualifications such as the training and certification required to fulfilling your specific dream, God will ensure that people qualify you as well. You do not need man's acceptance or approval to start following your dream. Your dream is a part of your purpose, and no one has the authority to tell you that you are not good enough for it.

How Do You Dress?

The reality is that other people will always size you up. The first thing they take note of is usually your attire; the second thing they are curious about is the way you speak. These two things, can tell them within the first two seconds of encountering you, whether or not they are going to be interested in anything that concerns you. Whether you are on the job, on an assignment or just randomly walking through a grocery store, people are watching. People watch other people, this is how we grow and develop as human beings.

I was once speaking to a young lady who expressed to me that there is no real culture in America today. Everyone is trying to be like everyone, and the culture is a culture of copying other people. We are all guilty of mimicking others in some kind of way; reason being, there is an American Standard, and an ideal dress code called professionalism. Globally this is an acceptable way of dressing for everyone.

A professional dress code usually consists of a suit, dress slacks, complementing shoes, neutral makeup and mild accessories. I believe professional dressing makes you credible to a degree. It lets others know that you're trustworthy and serious. Even though professional dressing puts you in a box with the rest of the world, you can still have fun with your uniform or attire. If you're going to be professional, you can create your own style of professionalism that is acceptable for whatever type of dream or work you are pursuing. Whatever you wear, ensure that you are confident and content with it. Know that you have checked and double checked your image to your liking, prior to walking out the door. Keep in mind, your opinion of yourself is what really matters.

When you feel confident in the way you look, you will be confident in your work, even as you're speaking to others. People usually know a confident person when they see one. Remember, the world accepts professionalism and you can uniquely tailor your professional image to your liking.

I remember talking to a friend one day, and I asked her if she liked the shoes I was wearing. She replied by asking me if I liked them, I said "Yes," her next response was: "If you like them, why are you asking me?" Instead of taking offense to this, I got excited because she helped me to understand that I really shouldn't care about her opinion, or anyone else's for that matter. The truth is when you seek acceptance and approval from others; you will see that people all have different standards.

On another occasion, I was speaking with a few of my friends about my hair and how I should wear it. One of them said she likes it when it is long and curly, another friend expressed that she likes the short angled bob look on me. Getting both of these opinions really confused me, simply because, I enjoy both looks when they fit certain occasions. Please! Do not live your life trying to be accepted by others. If you do, you will always question yourself according to your assumed thinking of other people's perceptions of you. Even when you know people are sizing you up, pay no attention to it; remain confident.

How Do You Speak?

Some of us are disqualified because of the way we speak. I know for me personally, I've always been very nervous about how my speech is received by others. I've had people tell me that I have a very soft girly voice and I've also had others say that I come across harsh. Sometimes when we go to speak to people, we are worried that we sound uneducated, too country, or too urban, some of us are even worried that we project too much of a fake proper tone.

All these things are a part of the battle within our minds. This battle is called fear, it can be easily annihilated if it is ignored and substituted for faith. On the other hand, if you are one who wants to tune up on your speech so that people can receive you in the way that you desire, then you should position yourself for criticism. I believe you will gain confidence, especially when you know you have received correction for proper speaking. Your interview skills will be sharper, and your approach to people will always be accepted.

The way you speak will start to get opportunities that lead you into fulfilling your dream. When these things start happening, you will have a tingle in your stomach that says 'I'm not ready'. This sensation can be interpreted by your mind as a joyous fear; it will make you feel excited and nervous all at the same time. For some of us, we get sweaty arm pits, sweaty hands and stuttering of our words. When this happens it's your body's way of telling you that your dream is about to begin. The moment you've been waiting for has now arrived, brace yourself and get ready for what's about to happen next. This really is a great place to be; even if you feel fear, it's a good thing. Just remember that the only people you want to strive to impress is God and yourself. Do not allow your mind to work against you or to tell you anything contrary to the truth.

Peer Pressure

Many of us have peer pressure which can lead to the fear of being accepted. Even adults experience peer pressure, which is usually on another level of seriousness, this is because of the realistic moves that need to be made. This peer pressure begins in the mind of the victim. As a result of fear, we submit our actions according to what we believe the people around us will accept. There is no right or wrong way of being you and doing things according to the way you choose to do them.

It is true that peer pressure is real; people are constantly being judgmental about things that really don't matter. We need to get it in our minds that peer pressure is one of the main triggers for fear in both children and adults. Sometimes, we even accept peer pressure from those who have not actually pressured us about anything. Our assumptive mind tells us that this person is a certain way, and they will not respect our decisions. We jump to conclusions; if we know a person's character, we can automatically predict their views of us. Whatever you do, don't let your assumptive mind talk you out of your dream.

Executive Decision Maker

When you are fulfilling your dream, you cannot allow too many people to give an opinion about the things that you are doing. When you extend the opportunity for others to give their opinion, somewhere along the line you may lose your original vision along with your own opinion. I believe, when it comes to the decisions that need to be made about certain things regarding your dream, you ought to be the executive decision maker. Reason being, when you start to let other opinions into the picture, your view becomes clouded and you become robbed of your authority on the matter. If this happens, it could be very hard to come back and regain control after that point.

Some people will try to give you their opinion just because they want a say in the outcome. They want to be able to tell people they did it for you, and you would not have completed it without them. Someone might want to help just so they can take the credit for your dream. Just be wise when you are getting any type of help or opinion from anyone else. It's really sad, but there are people that will go so far as to say they made you; even though they know they did nothing for you. It's unfortunate but this will happen and you must be very careful to not lose your executive authority over your dream. Remember that you are the sole founder and CEO of your dream; no one can take that from you.

No Longer Embarrassed

Sometimes our dreams are hindered on account of remembering things from the past that embarrassed us. Your past has everything to do with what you learned and where you're going. No one can hold anything over you that God has forgiven you for. There could be some things that you haven't confessed to yet. If so understand that they are feeding the shame and embarrassment that you may be feeling. There's no need to ask for forgiveness of sin, because when you belong to Jesus Christ, His request is that you just confess.

1John 1:9 says *"if we confess our sins God is faithful and just to forgive us our sin and to cleanse us of all unrighteousness."*

People Who Are Not Released Yet

In church environments some people genuinely desire to pursue the call to ministry over their life. If this is your desire ", and you fear being rejected by your leader," I would advise you to make sure that you're ready and prepared to go forth. Within yourself, God will give you a release, which is your golden ticket to go out and fulfill your calling. Usually, you feel this release when someone else has released you. Even Jesus was not released into ministry until His encounter with John the Baptist. Somebody reading this book feels a release from God into your ministry; maybe the ministry that you are under cares nothing about the ministry that God has given you. Their desire and focus is on the ministry that God has given them. Maybe you've been there for a while and they have given you years of empty promises. Understand that it is not the will of God for you to be manipulated, used or spiritually frustrated. Do not become frustrated because your timing is not Gods timing. The word of God says:

Ecclesiastics 3:1 *"To everything there is a season and a time to every purpose under heaven."*

This lets me see that God already knows the beginning and the end of every situation. Sometimes when you sit on a gift, or a ministry too long you become frustrated, and start to seek ungodly outlets; before you know it you're completely bottled down in sin. This type of frustration can leave you feeling so far from walking in your purpose that you begin to forget the very call of God on your life.

Spiritual Frustration

For a long time I was unfulfilled, even though I knew a part of my calling, I was not released so I became spiritually frustrated. When I was 19 the Lord Jesus called me into ministry. I thought I was good to go, even though I knew nothing more than what John 3:16 had to offer. 6 years went by. I sat and eventually began to lose sight of the original calling.

One day, I prayed a prayer and I asked God why things were not happening like I knew they should be. The Lord expressed to me that He was waiting on me. He released me two years prior to that prayer, but I was not sensitive enough to take those opportunities.

Sometimes God sends us our Moses, and because we are so focused on what we can't do, we miss the opportunities that He put directly in front of our faces. When I began to accept that God was moving me into my purpose, I looked at the waiting period differently. When you set your heart out to do the work of God, know that it is not too late, because there is a due season and God will honor you with every blessing.

Galatians 6:9
"Let us not be weary in well doing: for in due season we shall reap if we faint not."

Even if you are advanced in years; it is never too late, God needs your wisdom and experience in His kingdom.

Furthermore, there are people that are waiting on you to give them the piece to their puzzle, so that they can go forward and walk in their purpose.

Fear of Families Opinions

Many of us have family members we love with all our hearts. Naturally the opinions of your family will mean everything to you. If you have a bad reputation with your family, this can cause you to be scarred and distant toward people. In this broken state, it is very hard to fulfill your dream, because the people who are supposed to believe in you are the main ones trying to tear you down. When you've made a mistake or you've lived a life that you regret, your family will be the first to remember and throw it in your face. This is discouraging altogether, you must understand how to handle the fear of your family's opinion before you can truly step into your purpose.

Where it began

When I was 19 I rededicated my life to the Lord. I was very excited about my newfound relationship with God. I had such a joy because I knew that I truly had him, I could feel His gentleness and His love all over me. I was sure without a shadow of a doubt that I was in a covenant relationship with the Lord Jesus Christ, and no one could tell me otherwise.

As hungry as I was for God, I needed more. So the elders spoke to me about the baptism of the Holy Spirit with the evidence of speaking in other tongues. They said

He would give me power. I did not hesitate, I believed by faith and I was baptized that same day.

A Direct Invite

The Lord started to give me dreams of someday ministering to the world and encouraging people from all walks of life. I was filled with the Holy Spirit on December 28, 2008. Two nights before this, I received a dream from God which at the time I didn't know was a direct invitation from the Lord Himself. In the dream, the Lord was speaking to me among a group of about five others. We were situated in the kitchen at my job. As He was speaking He was informing us about the last days. He was sharing that He selected us for a particular mission; one of the things I remember Him saying was that we cannot forget that all of our possessions will be thrown into the whirlwind.

Then, the scene changed so that it was only Jesus and I. We were walking outside the job. As we were talking He was on my left and I was on his right side, it appeared to be nighttime, but there was a light shining on us that lit our path. He was giving me instructions about the task that He wanted me to complete. He was reassuring me that He would be with me throughout the whole ministry. This dream, was one of the most vivid dreams I have ever had, it became more of a reality every day after. I went to church that following Sunday and received the baptism of the Holy Spirit. All I knew was that this was amazing and I wanted everyone to experience the same thing. I felt clean and renewed; as far as I can remember it was probably the most beautiful day of my life.

Just like any other person who would be excited about their gift, I went and shared the good news with my family first. Back then I didn't feel like my family was nearly as excited as I was. This really hurt my feelings, I wasn't even sure if I wanted to continue on with the plan of God for my life. Everyone else seemed to be excited for me. The people at my job and the church were happily rejoicing with me.

Though I needed their love and support I did not let this discourage me. The fact that I was two hours away, gave me enough distance to concentrate on my new relationship with the Lord. Now, my family is very supportive of my role in the kingdom of God. I can feel the love, reverence and respect they have for me. They have my heart, and it feels so good to have that balance of their love and support. I honestly feel like they strive to protect the anointing that is on my life when I'm around now. If this is you and your family is not on board with your plans, I encourage you to hang in there and keep praying; God will turn it around for you.

During the time that I was on this journey with the Lord, I had no one to look up to other than a woman from my job named Lola who is like a mother to me now. I didn't have cable so I couldn't watch Christian TV, the only thing I had for my personal development was the church, the bible, and Lola. God knew that this was enough for me, because if I did have access to Christian television, it probably would have confused my thoughts about the Lord, not because their preaching was wrong, but because I was merely a babe to this Christian thing. A babe is only able to contain milk, it is pointless feeding them meat when they cannot chew nor swallow. God knew exactly what I needed to ensure that my relationship with Him was not in jeopardy.

Here I am, a new Christian and now my dream is to spread the gospel of Jesus Christ, but I feared not being accepted. I felt ostracized and alone. I had no real friends because the friends that I was used to were all back in my hometown. I was afraid of gaining new friends because I feared being called crazy and weird, so I made myself unavailable and pretty much non-existent. One lady said she felt like I left the face of the earth. Sure enough I had a desire to be social and have fun, however, if that meant I had to endure being looked at in a negative way because of my radical desire for the things of God, I was okay with being alone. Sometimes that walk with God can have you in a place where you are ostracized and don't fully understand why, this is the wilderness experience that we all go through as believers.

My family became anyone who understood and supported the call of God on my life. I know this seems harsh, but if you are going to walk in your complete purpose, you cannot look at, or focus on the people who don't understand you. They must be cut off, and if you don't separate yourself in a timely manner, pretty soon their negativity can cause you to give up on the very call that God himself has called you to.

If you are one who has put your dreams on hold because your family is not supportive, but rather negative. I encourage you to occasionally take some time to yourself and be strong, so that God can nurture you and help you fulfill your dreams and ultimately your purpose. Don't worry about the negative words that they

47

will say, because in the end when you are on your dream cloud, the same ones who tried to tear you down will be the ones asking you if they can join you. You should always remain loving to everyone, but being to close at the expense of your peace should never be compromised.

The fear of acceptance comes after the best of us, but we must keep in mind that weather or not people accept your dream you are still required to fulfil your purpose in life. If you connect with the lord and welcome His leading you will find that the blows of life will not hurt as bad. Get excited and know that you don't need to be accepted by man to feel validation concerning your dreams.

Chapter 5

Fear of Shame and failure

Adam and Eve

Sometimes I see people afraid to step out on faith and pursue their dreams simply because of the fear of shame and rejection. It doesn't matter what you have done in your past you have every right to pursue your dream and live a meaningful life just like the rest of the sinners in the world. The fear of shame and rejection was first displayed in:

> **Genesis 3:7-10 "The eyes of both of them were opened, and they knew that they were naked; and they sewed fig leaves together and made themselves coverings. And they heard the sound of the Lord God walking in the garden in the cool of the day so Adam and his wife hid themselves from the presence of the Lord God among the trees of the garden. The Lord God called to Adam and said to him where are you? So he said I heard your voice in the garden and I was afraid because I was naked so I hid."**

They were afraid of what He would say, how He would look at them, and how He would treat them. Their fear of being rejected by God is what caused them to hide. This is naturally what we do when we are afraid and fearful of rejection. We close ourselves up to the people that love us the most, and we live our lives in secret. This feeling of shame and rejection was very new to Adam and Eve; the most logical idea was to hide.

Some of us, if not all of us, have had a similar experience like that of Adam and Eve. Dwelling in shame, can hinder our dream in so many ways. Sitting under the ministry of Dr. David C Forbes Junior, really helped restore me back to my rightful place in God. This is where I managed to shed off the majority of the guilt and shame I was carrying. At the time he was teaching about grace and love and not being ashamed. Every day I was declaring that I was the righteousness of God in Christ Jesus. If it wasn't for Columbus Christian Center's church, I would not be where I am today. I received healing and restoration through love and lots of hugs when I attended this church. Even though I was ashamed and felt like people could tell, I pressed my way through because I knew that God had something there for me. In less than one year, I felt like the bruised and broken woman became the beautiful blessed woman. For this reason I am forever grateful for Dr. David and Tracy Forbes.

Weakness to Overcome

I recall being in a heartbreaking relationship that almost stole my dream and even my relationship with God. This was one of the hardest things to recover from; especially when I put my trust in the one who I would have never expected to bring me that much pain. Many nights I cried myself to sleep, in the midnight hour I would pray and ask God to heal my heart. Deep within I could feel the painful wounds bleeding continually. That awful experience tried to rip me to pieces. This is when I knew that the enemy was truly after my soul. Looking back on it, I could tell he wanted to stop me before I got started.

Some churches feel like if you mess up, you automatically lose the respect of everyone and the love of God and that there is nothing you can do to recover. This is simply not true; God is on your side and loves you unconditionally. The lost son in Luke 15:11, left home and destroyed his life but when he was reunited with his father, he received more in his humble return than he did in his wicked departure. With that being said, we must understand that there is nothing you can do to get God to turn his back on you unless you renounce Christ. This is the reason why Jesus gave us this parable. He brought you here not to turn his back on you but because He has an amazing purpose for your life. Being shameful and regretful will keep you bound until you decide enough is enough.

No More Hiding

So if you are one who is in hiding because of your past, and unable to start your dreams; as your sister in Christ I encourage you to tell the truth and confess. If you are not first honest with yourself, you can't be honest with others, and you will walk around feeling shame and regret having your outside dressed to impress and you're inside empty.

Some of us have too much to lose, our name, our reputation and our children's respect, so we hide as much of our wrong doings as possible. But one thing that we must understand is that there can never be an unfixable mistake. When you are comfortable with telling your wrongdoing to people, this means you do not care what they think neither do you live in fear of rejection, but you are free from the opinions of others. Everyone knows it is better to keep the secret from the world because when the world gets ahold of any type of dirt on you, they will use that dirt to destroy you any way they can. Being ashamed and afraid of what the world will think is not wise, because by trying to please the world and fit in, you make yourself an enemy to God. Jesus said a friend of the world is an enemy to God.

Jesus *said "if the world hates you, you know that it hated me before it hated you."* John 15:18

For this reason, my desire is not to impress the world but to live in freedom and liberty. By sharing things about myself, I'm hoping that somebody else will be inspired to get free like I did when I first started confessing. When Shame and the fear of rejection no longer intimidate you, you are free to share your story and pursue your dreams how you wish. Not only that but we should keep in mind that God does not carry grudges against those who are in Christ Jesus. I make a conscious effort not to walk according to the flesh but according to the spirit of God. I am not under the law nor am I under man's opinion, but I am under God's Grace. If God has forgiven you, you have to forgive yourself. The Bible says in:

1 John1:9 "If we confess our sins, he is faithful and just to forgive us our sins and to cleanse us from all unrighteousness."

So here we have it, genuine confession and knowing that you are forgiven for anything that you have done, can release you from the shame and fear of rejection. When God came to Adam and Eve, the first thing that they did was tell God what happened, their confession along with God's covering enabled them to come out of hiding and be free to move on with their lives. If you are one who has hid behind Shame of something you have done, I'm encouraging you to take the next step, confess and be free, God will cover you, and remember it is none of your business what others think of you. Your life's purpose depends on it.

Failure

Failure is a word that can feel like a threat to people with fear. Failure is something that we all face when we are pursuing our dreams, there defiantly will be times during the process that you feel like you failed. In order to feel failure, there must first be some sort of goal or intended objective that you set your mind to complete. The fear of failure is to entertain an intense anxiety in pursuit of a goal or mission.

Gideon feared defeat and failure so much that it got to the point where he thought he was getting on God's nerves. Gideon was doubtful on his first encounter with his destiny. In Judges 6:5 the angel tells him that God is with him, Gideon asked the angel how it could be possible, when God's people were in bondage. Where are the miracles which we heard from our fathers? Certainly God has forsaken us and delivered us into the hands of the Midianites.

It looks like God wanted him to bring this up, because in the next paragraph, God says speaking of the Midianites I have called you to go and save Israel. Immediately, in verse 15 Gideon starts to doubt again and enters into the fear of failure, he asks "how can I save Israel? You know that my clan is the weakest in Manasseh, and I the least in my father's house." In other words, he was telling God that he wanted the least person of all Israel to do the biggest task. Gideon considered his rank and his popularity, but God was considering his purpose. God tells him "I am with you and you will defeat the Midianites as one man."

Give Me a Sign

Gideon started to fear that he would fail, so he asked God to show him a sign that it was He who was talking. Not only did he begin to doubt the task that he was commissioned to do, but he doubted the very person that he was talking to. Many of us do this when God instructs us or gives us a vision, not only do we doubt the vision, but we doubt that it was even God who gave us the vision to begin with, especially when we consider the things that are coming against us.

God gave him the first sign by consuming the unleavened bread and the meat on the rock. The second sign was in verse 25 when God did not allow him to be killed after he destroyed the altar of Baal. This was a big deal because everybody worshiped Baal, including Israel. So for him to tear down the altars meant that he was supposed to die. The third sign was the fleece; he asked God to make the threshing floor dry and the fleece wet. God did as Gideon requested so that Gideon could know that it was God who chose him, he then reversed his request and asked God to now make the fleece dry and the threshing floor wet, so God did as Gideon requested so that again, Gideon could know that it was God who chose him.

The fourth sign that God gave Gideon was in judges 7:13-14, God knew that Gideon was fearful of failure, so he decided to allow him to overhear the conversation of a man who had a dream. This man was telling his dream to his friend, not knowing that the dream was about Gideon, the other man interprets the dream and lets them know about the dream.

Gideon overhearing this conversation is now full of faith even after all of the firsthand signs that God gave him. His faith did not come from talking with the angel of the Lord, his faith did not come after being spared from death, and his faith did not come through the wet and dry fleece. His faith came when his heart was strengthened after he heard the conversation and understood that the people viewed him as a conqueror.

What Others Think Shouldn't Matter

Was there ever a time when God told you some sort of truth about yourself and shown you time and time again with signs and wonders, but you wouldn't believe it until somebody gave you a shout out or showed you recognition? This is why you see people who will do nothing unless other people approve of it. The success of your dream should not be determined by the people who approve or disapprove of you.

I believe Gideon knew God would deliver him, but he needed to know that he had the support of people. Somehow you know that you are walking in your calling and your purpose, but it doesn't hit you until you see your face on TV, in a magazine or on the cover of a book. If we are not careful, validation from others can be the determining factor of whether or not we pursue our purpose. What other people think of you should not be your concern.

A Dreamer's Imagination

Dreams first began in our imagination. When we surround ourselves around people who have no dreams, it causes us to stop dreaming altogether. Most of the time, when people fear failing they will often choose to not continue on with their plans. Some people have dreams that they desire to pursue, but because of their fear of failing mixed with their fear of what others will think of them, they let their dreams die.

At first, all you saw was the dream, the finish line and the trophy, but the minute you became fearful, you thought of everything that could go wrong. You said to yourself maybe this is not a good idea, it might be too risky, I could break a leg, my rent is coming up maybe I should just wait. In the beginning, your main focus was the big picture, you saw it and were determined that you were going to get it because your commitment to it was serious, but then suddenly you saw the bad picture and you started to freak out, you took a step back and wondered if it was ever supposed to come to pass in the first place.

Dream haters on your dream cloud

One person in particular who had no fear of failure was Joseph. Here he is sharing his dream with the people who were supposed to support him and his gift. Because his brothers are not dreamers, they immediately tried to stop his dream. Not everyone cares about your dream, but if you give your focus and dedication to your dreams, eventually people will join you on your cloud. Some of us have people around us who are very afraid of our dreams but this is no reason to fear.

I believe a dream is a deposit from heaven into the bank account of your mind, which gives you the ability and the insight to make it visible here on earth. Some of us have people in our lives that we love who happen to be very negative and jealous hearted. Some of these people are brothers, sisters, aunts, uncles, cousins, and even parents. Sometimes when we esteem people with high regard and respect, we take their views and opinions as our own. Therefore, if someone doesn't agree with your dream, it is easier to immediately invest in the fear of failure.

Fear of Death before the promise is fulfilled

Abraham was a prime example of a man who feared death. Abraham says to his wife:

> **Genesis 12:12 – 13 *"Therefore it will happen, when the Egyptian see you,***

> **that they will say, this is his wife; and
> they will kill me, but they will let you
> live. Please say you are my sister that it
> may be well with you for your sake, and
> that I may live because of you."**

Abraham lied and convinced Sarah to lie so that he would not be killed. He knew that he was walking into a death trap and wanted to ensure he escaped. Abraham had every reason to be fearful of death, it seemed as though it ran in his family. His brother Haran died before his father Tarah then his father died in the land of Haran. As you look at his life, you can tell that he was not a big fan of death. Not only did he lie to spare himself from death, but he also intercedes for lot his nephew in Genesis 18.

I believe this is one of the reasons why God tested Abraham like he did. To instruct him to kill his son was the ultimate test of faith. He tested him in the area he feared the most in order to birth out the promise of Jesus Christ. I believe sometimes God leads us into the thing we fear the most to bring out the promise that he has given us.

Family Fears

Death is something that no one wants to talk about. Most of the time, the reason that death can seem so tragic is because of the way people die. We see people dying in car accidents, shootings, fires, and natural disasters. Another reason for why death is so tragic is because it is literally a permanent change of address, and no one likes the idea of leaving Earth for good. The wonderful thing about being a believer of the Lord Jesus Christ is that when we die, it's really not death. In fact death for us it is reversed to life. Our life has not ended when we die. By no means has it ceased but it has just begun.

> **John 11:25, 16 *"Jesus said unto her I am the resurrection and the life: and he that believes in me, though he was dead, yet shall he live: and whosoever live and believes in me shall never die."***

So there we see it, the way to eternal life is to believe in Jesus Christ while we are living. There is no escaping death; everyone has to face it at some point in time, but this should not be an excuse for not going after your dream

If you are destined to pursue your dream, just know that God will take care of your life. Do not be afraid of death because it has already been appointed onto every man.

> **Hebrews 9:27 says *"and as it is appointed for man to die once, but after this comes judgment."***

A Heavenly Vision

Those of us that are in Christ have nothing to fear because just like Paul said in:

> **Philippians 1:21 *"For me to live is Christ and to die is gain."***

Paul understood that by leaving this earth he would be with his Lord forever. I don't know about you, but I have sometimes felt an urgency to meet the Lord and to be in heaven with him. Some people would mistake this as a suicidal thought, but in fact it is quite the opposite. When you picture yourself spending your whole life with someone you love and admire, you look forward to the day that this dream can become a reality, you no longer become fearful of death, but you become hopeful for the day that you meet the love of your life. This is why you see so many of the prophets of old facing death like it's a breeze, and wearing persecution like it is a badge of honor. One of my favorite pieces of Scripture is revelation 21 and 22, where it talks about heaven and describes the New Jerusalem. It is such an encouraging ending; and. the description helps us to imagine the streets, the walls, the lighting and much more.

The Perfect Life

Sometimes I sit back and dream about Heaven and how beautiful it's going to be that day, I think about how everyone will be on one accord with no strife among us. We will all laugh together and it will always be something to giggle about and something to be happy for. We will be living in the joy of the Lord eternally; I like to think of it as the perfect life, the life that God established for us in the beginning before the fall of man.

Now if you're not careful you will encounter evil spirits that like to rub off on you just to put you in a bad mood, and to mess with your destiny; this is not the will of God for our lives. It's very possible for us to have those moments of perfection here on earth when we are gathering our thoughts in prayer, communicating with Him as if He's right there and imagining life in its completion.

I remember being in church one day and the Lord gave me a beautiful vision, I will never forget the way that it came to me. We were all sitting before the throne of God and our alignment was like the perfect army. I saw that we were kneeling before the throne. As we were worshiping God, I saw a physical manifestation of His glory passing through all of us. It looked like the line was uncountable and He started by shooting His glory and the fullness of His being through the first row of people. It became like a wave moving down the line from person-to-person. Sometimes when I think about this vision it brings tears to my eyes and gives me hope for something greater.

In His Presence

If you have never experienced the presence of God, then it is likely that you will not understand what I'm saying. I will admit that the presence of God is better than any earthly pleasure that we will experience during this life. I am excited about the day that I get to be with my Lord in that glorious atmosphere feeding and living off of his presence. In the vision it looked like that was how he fed us, as though it was our daily food. It was what kept us alive. When we are caught up in the goodness of God there are no sad days. So when you have been given a vision like this, how could you not desire to be with the Lord for real? The vision was so real to me that I had to get up in front of the church and tell the vision just as I saw it. The rejoicing that went on that day was amazing.

We pictured ourselves in a never ending party playing in the presence of God.

Earlier I talked about how we should always use our imagination. God deposited this vision into my imagination. I still get excited whenever I envision it again. Sometimes when I get sad, depressed or lonely I think about the vision of heaven and it instantly brightens my soul. Suddenly I have the desire to continue on with my dreams with joy and gladness of heart. So why fear death? Why not embrace it when you know where you're going?

If this is you who's afraid of death and you want this type of vision for yourself, I encourage you to believe in the Lord Jesus Christ and turn away from your sin so you can also experience the hope and promise of heaven. It will enable you to fulfill your purpose knowing that you have a great ending whether Jesus shows up today or tomorrow. God would never take away your freedom of choice, nor would He force you to accept him or to stay with him. You have a choice of whether or not you want to do well in the site of the Lord. Life on earth has nothing on life in heaven, I've heard stories of people that have gone to heaven and returned to earth and I am yet to hear any of them say that it was a terrible vacation. I believe God gives us a taste of his goodness so that we don't lose sight of the great thing he has prepared for us.

The fear of death can ultimately put a pin in your dream so that your dream can go nowhere. If this is you, and the enemy has told you that he is going to kill you and that you will never fulfill your purpose or your dreams, then you need to tell him that you're not dying anytime soon because it is God who holds the key to life-and-death. Now go your way and get started on your dream, just know that to make you fearful is a part of the enemy's job. I heard my friend Lisa St. Jean say that she is not afraid of the devil because he has his own job to do. He's going to do his job and I'm going to do my job. His job is to come after me and my job is to unleash Jesus on him.

Chapter 6

A Dream Declares War

When people have a dream, what they are really saying is that they are declaring war. If you have a dream, it means that you are going to go against your current mediocre lifestyle along with various other opposing forces. Moving forward in your dream is almost the same as stepping on the battlefield. Before you pursue it, your mind has to be prepared for battle in its entirety, whatever that may be. Your battle may be removing people from your life who could literally annihilate your dream. Your battle may even be a faith battle, where you literally have to stand on everything that you believe to be true so that you can fulfill your dream and ultimately achieve your purpose.

The Vision Belongs To You

Don't let other people dictate your dream. You know the dream that is inside of you, you know what it looks like, what it sounds like and even how it feels. You're the only person who has a visual of what your dream is supposed to look like. God gave it to you and not to them because it isn't for them, it's for you. Every part of your dream represents a desire on the inside of your heart, and eventually you'll start to understand more about yourself as you pursue it. I don't like it when I'm speaking with someone, and begin to tell them the desires of my heart and all of a sudden they start to rebuke me. This happened one time and the Lord help me to understand that "they are rebuking you because I gave the vision to you and not them."

How can you expect someone to see a vision that's invisible to everyone else except for you? So please save yourself discouragement and don't mention it. There's always someone waiting to tear down your dream cloud so that you cannot be on display. Some people genuinely believe they are giving you the right advice by secretly hinting that it's not a good idea. These are the types of people that I never mention my dream to, at least not until it's almost finished.

For some reason, humans love to give unwanted opinions in places that they feel necessary. Because of that reason, I'm strongly encouraging you to not share your dream with everyone. Now if something is about to happen with your dream, such as you got the loan and you are very excited about it, then it is in your best interest to share it as it's unlikely that people will rebuke excitement and good news.

God Supporters

By no means am I telling you to run from rebuke, this is because sometimes rebuke can be a good thing. It can be the very thing that protects you during the process of fulfilling your dream. It is very important for us to have someone who holds us accountable to our dream and who is also very excited about it. Maybe this person is a mentor, friend or family member. I know for me that person is my mentor Shelly Martin. She supports me even at speaking engagements, she holds me accountable for being on-time and keeping my marketing materials on hand. Be sure that this person has no personal vendetta against you as not everyone has your best interest at heart

Make sure that there is someone there to keep you focused and to provide encouragement, someone who wants to see your dream come to pass just as much as you do. Don't get discouraged by what people will say to you or about you. People talking about you should never be your motivating factor for fulfilling your dream, because at that point you're no longer doing it for you, but for the naysayers. Keep in mind that your dream will bless the right people and God will start to send people to uplift and support you as you fulfill your dreams. I thank God for my friend Lisa who was very encouraging when I was writing this book. I explained to her I have so much in me that I needed to get on paper and I only had 60 days to do it. She would call me and sometimes we would talk about our dreams and how we can complete them. I recall receiving a tremendous amount of encouragement from her.

On your journey to fulfilling your dream, you cannot allow your circle to be filled with people who are intimidated by it. I've had people who I thought were for me and excited about the things that God was doing in my life, but all the while they were secretly praying against me. This is why you must not forget that when you begin to dream out loud, what you are really saying to the opposing forces is that you want war. Though opposition is normal you must always have a battle plan for your success.

If you have someone who you feel is pretending to care about you and your dream, then you may need to consider cutting that person out of your circle before you get to your dream cloud. As you go along and fulfill your dream, God will start to reveal to you those people were truly for you. He will start to send people your way whom you have dream connections with.

Relationship Distractions

Some of us let distractions come into the picture, distractions that have nothing to do with our dream. Relationship distractions for example, are the best ammunitions for destroying a dream. If you are not careful, you will not understand that your relationship and your marriage can be the very thing that takes you completely off course and will make it difficult for you to rebuild your entire dream. Some of us get connected with men and women who really don't care about us let alone our dream. Most of the time, they want to use you for their own pleasures and benefit when it's convenient for them. So when you talk to them about your dream it's almost like you're blowing dust in the air, it means nothing. They can't be excited for you because they don't care about you.

When I was in a relationship with a man who I thought would help me fulfill the call of God on my life, I later realized that he had an ulterior motive. Had I known that I would get so hurt in that relationship beforehand, I wouldn't have allowed myself to get distracted in the first place. When it was all over I realized that he did not care about me, therefore, my dream and my purpose meant nothing to him. When we make decisions using wisdom it can save us a handful of heartache.

When David was dancing before the Lord, he had one goal which was to please God. He danced so much that he didn't notice that his clothes were falling off his body, and then one of his wives came to tell him that he should be ashamed of himself for exposing his nakedness like that. She didn't understand that David's purpose was not to pay attention to how embarrassing he looked, but it was to glorify God with the gifts that God had given him.

Sometimes it's the people that are right underneath your nose. The ones you sleep with at night, that you think would want the best for you, but in reality they want nothing for you. This type of discouragement coming from the spouse may not be intentional. You may feel that this person does not believe in your dreams because they're not as supportive as you would like them to be. It may not be that the person is not supportive intentionally; it may have everything to do with the fact that they genuinely do not know how to celebrate others.

I used to know someone who did not know how to celebrate other people. She didn't know how to say anything positive such as 'I'm happy for you, that's good, how wonderful'. I couldn't understand what her problem was, but then one day it hit me and I realized that she really truly did not know how to rejoice with those who rejoice. If it wasn't her good news, she didn't know how to celebrate with me for my good news. This type of person is what you call a frenemy, they're not quite for you but they are not totally against you. Maybe you've never had any sort of run-in with them but at the same time they appear to be very nonchalant about anything that concerns you.

Spousal Support is important

When you encounter these people, you cannot give them too much of your dream because when you start to tell them about it, their responses will be so bland that you will begin to question how valuable your dream really is. Even though they mean no harm it is in your best interests to spare as little details as possible. For some of us this can be our husband or wife. If you are in a relationship with a person like this and you're not sure of what to do, you must keep in mind that your dream was entrusted to you. You cannot be disappointed about anyone's lack of support, remember your dream is your responsibility.

Some people feel that this is a just cause for a divorce or separation. But this isn't always necessary because of a simple lack of communication. Now I do believe that if one has a dream that is completely opposite from the person that they married or are in a relationship with, then that person needs to reconsider if their spouse is allowed on their dream cloud. When you're fulfilling your dream, depending on what it is, you can't afford to have people around you who are going in a completely different direction. If your dream is to move in with God, but your spouse's dream is to move in with the devil then you have a huge problem.

That's a bit extreme but I wanted to give you a broad example. On another hand, you have a dream of becoming a gospel singer but your spouse hates music and furthermore hates God. What do you do? How do you handle this type of rejection when you know that your dream is burning within you? I believe that these types of scenarios need to be addressed prayerfully. I would never tell anyone to leave their marriage, my advice is to always include Gods input and discretion. Understand that every ounce of negativity that you permit in your life as you're fulfilling your dream is going to feel equivalent to trying to grow a beautiful tree when someone keeps trying to chop it down. You may have a spouse who is not the least bit interested and is in fact against your dream, but you cannot let that stop you, because remember your dream is a link to your purpose.

My job is not to motivate you to believe that your dream will come without a battle or a struggle. Naturally we all want things to be easy and we get very frustrated when they're not. Most of us experience testing of our faith in most areas of our lives. Faith in God's says I believe that the Lord Jesus is real and that He is able to work all things out for my good. The Bible says in

> **Hebrews 11:6 "that without faith it is impossible to please God, for he who comes to God must believe that He is a rewarder of those that diligently seek Him."**

> **Matthew 17:20 "if you have faith as a mustard seed, you will say to this mountain, move from here to there, and it will move; and nothing will be impossible for you."**

You must have faith that when you set your heart out to complete your dream, it will happen for you. No matter what forces come up against you to make you fearful or to distract you it will happen as long as you believe it. Some of us get so far and then we start to doubt, like Peter for instance, as he walked on water he started to doubt it and when his disbelief started to rise, he started to fall... When I'm struggling with doubt I start to pray and connect with God, He then begins to renew my strength. Even when you don't believe in yourself, God believes in you and is always there to cheer you on. I have no doubt that when you set your mind and your heart out to complete your dream you will do it if you don't give up.

Distractions and Opposition

Keep in mind that when you set out to fulfill your dream you must always be prepared for war. Distraction has been one of the missiles fired at us by the enemy, which has had a huge impact on the timing of our breakthrough and blessings. When we know that we are being distracted we genuinely need to exercise our self-will over these situations. The wonderful thing about distraction and opposition is that they are usually temporary. When a person is distracted, it usually doesn't last that long, maybe a month, a year or two. In order for distraction to prevail against you, the enemy has to continue to distract you. Distraction is an indirect blow that has to be renewed every so often. He can distract you with one thing today, and then when you overcome that thing tomorrow, he has to distract you with something else.

Usually the distraction occurs with something that is specific to your desires. He will use movies to distract you; there can be something within that movie that throws you off-course. He also uses the music industry, understanding that there is a spirit behind all music. He can strategically use the lyrics which can trigger things, and you can eventually be led astray. But it's all temporary because he knows that his distractions have an expiration date. It's a beautiful thing to see someone wake up from their distraction. It's like one day they are distracted and you wouldn't think they would snap out of it, but the next day they come to their senses and they say to themselves "What was I thinking? I need to get back on track today!" When this happens the enemy says "Oh my! He's waking up, we have to hurry up and find something else to distract him with."

Let's say you were supposed to meet with someone one day but got distracted along the way. That distraction caused you to be late and miss your appointed opportunity. Unfortunately this has happened to all of us at some point in our lives. Some of us battle distraction more than we do fear. So again the good thing about distraction is that it is only temporary and comes with an expiration date. The bad thing about distraction is that it can cause a delay on your finances, your business, your relationships, your goals, and ultimately your dream.

Another disadvantage to distraction is the amount of enthusiasm is steals from us. Have you ever had a dream or a desire to do something and because you were distracted along the way you lost your zeal? By the time you make it to your dream or goal you are too drained to give it your complete effort. Some of us were so on fire for God, we were ready to start our ministry, and vision that He placed in our hearts, but by the time that ministry or dream was birth there was no more desire for the things of God. Some things you may still want to do, but by the time you come around to it, there's no more energy. You had all the energy you needed yesterday to complete this task but not today because you allowed yourself to be distracted.

Pursuing the Dream with No Energy or Zeal

Distraction also comes with a language; this is how you can detect your level of distraction. When you start making excuses for why you can't complete the tasks or dreams that you set your affections on, this is a lingo of distraction. 'I wish I could, maybe tomorrow, now is not the right time, who's going to help me? I'm just not ready, God knows my heart, I'm just not strong enough right now, I don't have the money, and one day I will get to it.' These are the words of a person who is currently distracted. Usually people who are distracted put their dreams on hold and they say 'for now I will leave this.' When the enemy hears that, it gives him more time to come up with ammunition to use against you. Remember your dream is war. His desire is to get you to a place where you are so distracted and fearful that you will never come back up with the same energy.

Distraction is designed to keep you off-course long enough for you to lose your zeal. Your zeal means everything to your dream. It is the gas that fuels you even when it looks like it's impossible. Distraction will cause you to approach the dream without excitement. Some people had dreams from years ago that they were passionate about, so passionate that when they talked about their dream, you could see the twinkle in their eyes. Now the opportunity of their dream coming to pass has stumbled upon them and because it has been so long, the fire for that dream has dwindled. It's like an NFL player who is about to play in the championship, he goes to the field, he has the uniform, he even has the fans on his side but he has no real energy. He was all hyped up for the game but his energy was stolen before he got there.

Opposition Brings Elevation

You must understand that if someone is coming against your dreams, all it means is that they are pushing you to fulfill them. The opposition is not coming to destroy you, but it is coming to elevate you to your next level. Whatever you do, do not be afraid of persecution that will arise as a result of you running after your dream, because without persecution you will never know how to persevere. Though your dream declares war on your mediocre life, you should look at your dream as your baby that you are sent to protect. No parent will allow anybody to hurt or harm their child. As a matter of fact, going by all the parents I know, if you even attempt to persecute their child, you will experience the wrath of that parent before you can even begin. It is up to you to guard and protect your dream with your life. No one is going to do it for you; it is your responsibility to be the overseer of your own dream.

If you protect your dream as you pursue your dream eventually your dream will reward you. It will be a testimony to your efforts that went forth to bring it into existence. I encourage you to not let anyone wipe your dream off the map. You have the key to your dream door and God has given you the responsibility of making sure no one breaks in to steal or to destroy it. Remember, when you face challenges they are only signs that God has more for you. Whatever you do, do not give into the 'woe is me' mentality.

You must never forget that you can overcome every obstacle-be it distraction or spiritual opposition because God has already equipped you with the necessary weapons to overcome every adversary. His word says in third John 2:3 beloved, I wish above all things that you may prosper and be in good health, will even as you're soul prosperous.

Chapter 7

Social media

Social media can be either a good thing or a bad thing for a person who has a dream that they desire to fulfill, this is because it can be used for your benefit, or it can be used to destroy you. You have it within your power to decide what role social media will play in your life, understand that as you become a public figure or leader you will have less and less control over your image. Social media is the easiest way to destroy everything that you have built and one of the fastest ways to build your life. If you truly want your dream to be a success you must not run from social media, but embrace all that comes with it.

Facebook

When I was 16, I joined the social media platform named Myspace; this gave me a good feel for what social media was all about. It wasn't until I turned 18 that I joined Facebook. I can honestly say through my own experiences that social media has never been a huge distraction for me; this is simply because I am not a fan of exposing my life to everyone. With my profile, I felt very much in control of what I wanted to share, and I was always aware of cyber bullying which was just as prominent back then as it is today. My main uses for Social media were to keep in touch with my friends and family and to sometimes post something funny or spiritual to my own profile page.

Nowadays, there is a lot more to being online, it is so easy to get wrapped up with what gets posted on social media sites like Facebook, that we could get lost spending four or five hours scrolling. When you allow your soul to get too consumed, you become addicted and open yourself up to all the forces that interact through Social media. Some of these forces are positive and other forces are negative.

Two-Faced

I believe social media is a two-faced system and some people are not fully aware of how both of those faces could impact their lives. By saying two-faced, I am referring to the different platforms that one can take on social media. You can take on either a personal platform, or a professional platform.

Personal Platform

I believe the personal platform is one of the most dangerous platforms to take. One of the reasons for this is because of the fact that every day you're exposing your intimate life with people, some you know and others you don't. Everyone who sets up a social media account must have a purpose, especially in this day and age; either you are going to get lost in the social media community or you will have a great impact.

All social media users must be aware of what they are posting so that they do not mislead people. If you are someone who others look up to, you cannot be seen with a drink or a drug in your pictures. This type of behavior is unacceptable on social media, especially for those who are striving to impact others in a positive way. However, unfortunately, this behavior has become the norm and it's really sad that children are on social media and have access to all of these things.

It seems as though this generation has no respect for the generations before us and the ones coming up after us. Whether you are fully aware of it or not, it is critical that you understand that social media is your mega phone to the world. It speaks about you loud and clear. For this reason, you cannot forget your purpose for being on social media. Everything must be posted as part of a purpose, if it's your personal life, then it needs to be shared without intimate or private details that you don't want others to throw back at you. Anything that comes after you post on social media is your responsibility, and if you use it inappropriately, then you must be able to take the consequences that come with that.

We must be serious about this thing. In the past, I have seen people put things on their page and feel confused when other people respond negatively towards what they posted; the reality is that no one would have responded back and it wouldn't have been talked about if that person hadn't fed it to them to begin with. Therefore, you should always know your purpose for using social media, and whether you post positive stuff, or personal stuff, there will always be people that will respond to everything you put out there.

We must be careful and watchful of others and their posts. I was speaking with one of my first cousins Aquarius one day and she mentioned that when she sees people who are posting negative things on Social media, she automatically sees it as a cry for help instead of looking at it from the perspective that most Social media users would. Some people can interpret this as a person being a drama queen but in reality they could be crying out. So the question is what is your purpose for social media?

What's The Purpose?

Nowadays everyone is contributing to the social media platform; you have governors and public officials who are also 'Tweeting' and 'Face-booking' along with the teenagers today. Social media is a thing of today, we see updates of Hollywood stars and various other famous people who post on Twitter, Instagram, and Facebook, the next thing we know is that they are appearing on a news channel all because they posted something that was taken out of context. You have to remember that everyone is watching your social media presence at all times and you have to control how you come across. If you forget your purpose, you will get lost in the social media world and it can get uglier than you originally intended.

Everything must be done with purpose, when you go to work you must have a purpose, when you tie your shoe lace there has to be a purpose; you eat your food because there is a purpose, when you communicate with people there has to be a purpose, the same goes with social media. The reality is that we do things consciously and unconsciously on purpose, but regardless of what this purpose is, we must remain in control.

If you have a personal platform you should keep in mind that by accepting anyone to be your friend on any social network, you are accepting the drama that comes along with that person as well. As soon as you click 'confirm' you expose yourself to that person, and in turn accept any nastiness that may come through on their profile. My hope is that you will start to see social media as an opportunity instead of an outlet. I am a firm believer that social media is not the place to vent when we are going through challenges in life. Furthermore, social media is not the cause of drama, the people that use it are! Anyone signed up to social media accounts will usually look to Social media for validation and advice. Social media cannot be your mentor, God is your mentor. For this reason Social media can be a dangerous world if it is not properly handled.

A Stalker's Playground

Through a personal platform we are not aware of how much information we actually give to strangers. Not everyone on social media is there for the right reasons and then there are people who carelessly give out information such as when they are going on vacation or that their parents have left them with a free house, this encourages all the wrong attention by giving strangers a first-hand insight on all of your moves. So if someone wanted to come and attack you or break into your home for example, they know exactly when no one else is going to be around to protect you or when your house is unoccupied. I think we forget that there are so many social media stalkers out there waiting for the perfect opportunity. My point is that if you are going to use social media make sure your being wise and using it to your advantage rather than letting it be someone else's advantage over you.

My intention is not to put a downer on social media networks because they can be the thing that saves a life; however it breaks my heart to see people suffering and getting robbed and killed because of their ignorance when using these platforms.

Professional Platform

A professional platform is perfect for someone looking to network and market. It is rare that you would experience cyber bullying when using social media on a professional basis, and you are far more likely to attract all of the right people, especially those who have a specific interest in what you are trying to market. Whether it's a business, ministry, or organization you are marketing, you have it within your control to make it what you want it to be.

Usually people respect a ministry or business in a different way because of the standards that they uphold. People are highly unlikely to go to your ministry page and post anything negative without good reason. If this were to occur, then it is clear that the person purposely went out of their way due to some sort of hatred rooted within. This is less likely to happen when you take a professional platform on purpose.

Regardless of the disadvantages, if you are someone who needs an influence through social media to pursue your dream, then there is really no way around it unless you hire someone to control all of your accounts with you. Nevertheless if you are starting a business, you are likely to need social media to help you with your dream. Without the presence of social media, you limit your revenue capacity. If your dream involves people, then you must take advantage of the benefits associated as it will give you access to marketing and networking for free.

There are also ways that you can expound your territory through paid advertising so that your professional platform gives you good exposure. There was a time when I wanted to get off of Facebook but I knew very little about Twitter and Instagram.

I remember a woman once reached out to me, she asked me to keep posting because I was encouraging her. That was the point I realized that my social media platform could not be taken lightly. This was the ministry that God entrusted to me for the edification of people all over the world and it could not be played with. After she messaged me, I began to see some of the people she was friends with had started to send me friend requests. This brings us back to making sure that we are posting on purpose.

I also recall a lady who sent me a message about a speaking opportunity. She said that she had been watching my page and even went through my posts from a year ago. After she witnessed how consistent and positive the things I posted were, she knew that I was the perfect candidate for her women's conference. She asked me if I could speak at an event and simply talk about how I evolved as a woman. This opportunity opened the door for me to begin speaking at various universities and conferences. So again when we post it must be on purpose, there are people who look up to you and expect a standard from you especially when there is a title before or after your name.

Addicted to Social Media Attention

I notice that there are a lot of insecure people using social media, some of which have a motive to boast about themselves just so others can see. When they get a new car it goes on Social media, when they get a new good paying job it goes on Social media. Everything they pose is to make people believe that their life is better than what it is. No longer do they aspire to be a unique individual because it is their desire, but they have been possessed by the spirit of pride that keeps them putting on a façade to impress their friends.

Truth is that human beings have a tendency to want to be popular and loved by all. If we would just live our lives and not concern ourselves constantly with the opinion of others, than we would truly have a more positive view about ourselves. Some social media users are addicted to the attention that comes along with their posts and their photos. When you reach a point where your popularity is derived from your sexual approach, the attention will become harder to reject. If we are not careful, we will look up one day and realize that we have sold our soul for a lost cause. It's sad to say the social media houses the souls of today's world.

So for those of us who yearn to fulfill your dream influence the next generation, we must keep in mind that our posting has to have a purpose. If you are there for the attention and the hype of it all you will miss your opportunity to make an impact on the world. If you are fulfilling your dream and social media is a part of that, everything you post will represent your name in the right way.

I was once called to speak at an event for women preachers. I was talking to one of my friends who normally travels with me for support; she and I had a conversation about the standards that we want to uphold. We spoke about how our appearance would be the first thing people would judge us for, so we wanted to make sure that we set the bar high for every appearance. If we dressed on purpose with class and integrity, people would associate that with our image.

The standard that I hold says I expect nothing less than Grade professional attire. Booty shorts are unacceptable, tight and nearly topless shirts I will not tolerate. The same goes for our social media presence; it should always be dressed in a way that people are not exposed to your nakedness. There should not be any form of profanity, or sexual exposure of any kind when we are posting on purpose. I am not endeavoring to dictate or control what people post on their social media accounts, but I aspire to help people understand some of the reasons why they breed this disrespect and heartache on social media. I'm hoping to coach you on how your influence is crucial to your dream.

If someone had the ability to write a book on all of the status updates, photos and videos that you have posted, how would that make you feel? Would you be ashamed or proud of what you have shared? Would you be embarrassed or honored? That's a question that most people don't consider as their posting. I remember for a while I could not post on Social media. As a Christian we should be cautious and prayerful whenever we put something out there for the world to see.

I remember creating posts on Facebook and I could feel the Lord leading me to erase the words that I had written. Keep in mind that I only desire to put inspirational content out there to edify people, but for whatever reason God was leading me to post nothing. At the time I didn't understand why I was so restricted with my posts. As we relate with the Lord we understand that he has his reasons for everything and that his ways are not the same as our ways.

Whether we know it or not, one day everything that we have done on this earth will have to be accounted for. There is a Scripture that talks about the book of remembrance.

> *Malachi 3:16 – 18 says "then thou who fear the Lord spoke to one another, and the Lord listened and heard them so a book of remembrance was written before him for those who fear the Lord and who meditate on his name. They shall be mine, says the Lord of hosts, on the day that I make them my jewel. I will spare them as a man spares his own son who serves him. Then you will again desire between the righteous and the wicked, between one who serve God and one who does not serve God."*

This Scripture is letting us know that when we fear God and talk about it with each other, there will be a book written to remember these things. There is a certain amount of mercy that you receive when you are careful with your words. If you are like me and you strive to please God daily, you are required to have a continual reverence and fear for God, which does not exclude your social media platform. The fear of God utterly justifies us and sets us apart in the eyes of the Lord. After encountering that Scripture, I understand everything I do must be on purpose. Even as you pursue your dream it has to be on purpose. In all of our endeavors we must always keep in mind that we are representing.

Represent Him Well

God will not stand for people who misrepresent him. Remember, he is the one who enables us to do all that we set our hearts out to do. When our social media accounts portray something contrary to God this means that we are misrepresenting him on so many levels. For those of us who have taken a ministers approach to social media, regardless of whether you have incorporated an organization or a business, the standard is higher. If we are not representing God in the right way this means that there is no real relationship. The Bible tells us what will happen in the last day,

> **Matthew 7:22 – 23 Jesus says *"many will say to me in that day, Lord, Lord, have we not prophesied in your name, cast out demons in your name, and done many wonders in your name? And then I will***

**declare to them, I never knew you: depart
from me, you who practice wickedness."**

If you are someone who practices wickedness, this means you make a conscious effort to go against the standards of God. Keep in mind that everything you do must be done with the right content and the right purpose. I believe that as you embark on this journey of fulfilling your dreams, God is going to start to reveal areas of your life that you need to surrender before your dream can genuinely manifest. Ultimately, his desire is to get you to fulfill your purpose, but if you do not know how to fulfill your dreams, it will be difficult for you to fulfill your complete purpose on this earth. Make sure you're using social media as an asset and not a liability, because if you have a social media account remember that it is also a puzzle to your purpose.

Chapter 8

How to Execute Your Dream

Let's Get Practical

Our dreams should be a big deal to us individually because your dream is something that you have the ability to birth on your own. If you are one who has a dream but don't understand how to really execute that dream, I want to share a few things with you that will help you make your dream become a reality in the near future. One of the first things we must keep in mind is that our dreams are only as real as we make them, there is no way we can expect someone else to come along and make our dream a reality first. You have to be the one to step up and say to yourself 'my dream is worth pursuing.' The truth is that no one else is going to care about your dream if you don't care about your dream. I'm going to give you nine things that you must have so that you can make your dream a reality. Though some of them might not pertain to your dream, but you will find that these principals are very important for everyone with a dream especially if you are starting your own business:

1. Cast your vision

2. Enthusiasm and confidence

3. Research and planning

4. Schooling and training

5. Formatting and presentation

6. Marketing and networking

7. Consistency and discipline

8. Staying focused

9. Setting a deadline

1. Cast Your Vision

To have a vision of your dream is like having a finished product or an imaginary prototype. Your vision helps you to stay focused while formatting and bringing it to fruition. Bringing it all together in your mind and putting it on paper gives you a defined view. You must be like God who knows the end from the beginning, so in the beginning you must write it down and create what you want the ending to look like.

> **Habakkuk 2:2 tells us "right the vision and make it plain on tablets."**

You might ask why it needs to be on tablets or paper. My answer to that is, when you write it out, it becomes established. For some reason as humans we are more prone to feel the need to complete something if it is written down rather than spoken or kept in our mind. Furthermore, it helps those around you to gage a clear view of how to execute this task. Some people depending on their dream see fit to go a step further and write down their mission which in reality what informs people of why they do what they do. So if you have a dream I encourage you to write an action plan and cast your vision as soon as possible.

2. Enthusiasm and Confidence

Enthusiasm is very important when it comes to pursuing your dream. Your enthusiasm is the life and the fuel to your dream. If your enthusiasm is low, the chances are that your dream will not come to pass as fast as you would like. You cannot be casual when you are pursuing your dream, the more aggressive you are the better. It's like a person who is so hungry that they know they will die if they don't eat. Your dream is your meal, it's your life and how you choose to survive. If you don't have the gas to do the legwork, there is no way you will see it come to pass like you desire.

When I say enthusiasm, I'm referring to your excitement and your passion about your dream. If you're not on fire to achieve it, no one else will do it for you. Throughout the whole process of pursuit you must stay passionate. A few things that can help you stay passionate are: constant research, praying, setting dates to make minor purchases and getting other enthusiastic people excited about your dream. You will discover that some people will not be excited about your dream but this is okay because God did not give the dream to them but to you. You should never allow anyone to discourage you concerning your dream. Your dream should be such a reality that you actually see it in its complete form.

I once had a similar conversation with a lady who really wanted to pursue her dream, but every time she starts to build momentum for it, she looks at someone else's achievement and immediately becomes discouraged.

This was her excuse for not pursuing her dream. I felt really sad for her because it meant that her dreams were contingent upon her emotions at the time. Don't let your dream suffer because your emotions can't fall in line. This is your time to pursue them once and for all, don't look back and don't get discouraged.

Confidence is a big deal for bringing your dream to pass. You must be confident when pursuing and presenting your dream to others. When you have a dream, everyone in the world around you become investors. People will respect your dream when they see your level of confidence in it. If you go to present your dream to a group of people and you have very little confidence, they will start to question if it's worth giving their attention.

Your confidents can be the determining factor of whether or not your dream will be a success. People don't often believe that what they have to offer is important. The crucial thing about confidence is that without it your dream is dead. If you don't have the confidence while you are presenting it to me, I won't have the confidence to invest. Even if you are unsure of whether or not your dream will be a benefit to a particular person, your lack of confidence would be robbing them of the opportunity to sample your dream at its best. The reality is that we all need each other so we must be confident in our dream whether it's a business, ministry or organization it is bound to be the solution to someone else's problem so stay enthusiastic and confident as much as possible.

3. Research and Planning
Research is a very important part of bringing your dream to pass. Research ensures that you dot all of

your I's and cross all your T's. Most people really don't care enough to complete this step because it can be very time-consuming and depressing. Sometimes when you research, you find more obstacles than opportunities. When you approach this, it should always be done with prayer. I've seen people get to this step and get discouraged which eventually causes them to give up on a dream. Reason being because the research has the ability to tell you whether your dream is worth it, affordable and realistic. When you start to research, you must keep in mind that your dream is already worth it.

Nothing should be able to detour you off of your dream, not even research. If you believe in it, have the enthusiasm and confidence about it, then there should be nothing able to separate you from seeing your dream come to pass. Your budget is going to be your sponsor as you fulfill your dream. While on this journey, you have to be strategic about your finances. Tell your money where it's going to go so that your dream can be as successful as possible. If you do not have a budget you are limiting your ability to maximize your dream potential. Your dream is only as big as your finances will allow. Don't be afraid to reach out to people to sponsor you, what I've found is that people don't mind sponsoring for a dream or a project that they believe in.

The amazing thing about research and planning is that it serves as a bulletproof vest that protects your dream. The more you know about how to pursue, build, and protect your dream the stronger and more secure it becomes. Sometimes the reason that dreams fall through or businesses fail is because there was a lack of research. Cost, budgeting, presentation and marketing are all areas that need to be thoroughly researched and planned out in order to ensure a bulletproof dream. Whatever you do, never discredit your research because that is what will tell you all the practical things you need to know about bringing your dream to pass. When I was writing this book, google was my best friend.

4. School and Training

If your dream requires you to attend school or some sort of training, it is very important that you consider the right one. If it is necessary to go to school, just know that when you come out you want to be ready to work and hit the ground running. Some of us dreamers really believe that we don't need to attend school or training, but what we fail to realize is that this is the most crucial part of fulfilling our dream. If you do not educate yourself first, you may find yourself in a terrible situation trying to make moves that you never knew existed, and doing things that you were unprepared for. You cannot rely on your natural abilities or just your spiritual gifts alone. Your abilities are naturally developed and are usually not directly given by God. Your skills and abilities are natural gifts; it could have been something that you were born with or something developed through experience and training. Even though your abilities and skills are naturally developed, God is still the one who enabled us. Allow yourself a window of time to train and develop yourself for your dream.

Whether we like to admit it or not, our dream will flow much smoother if we have the experience prior to jumping in the deep end. When you experience someone else doing it, it gives you faith.

5. Formatting and Presentation

Whether you are starting a product line, a stationary business or a ministry, the formatting and presentation is one of the most important steps for bringing your dream to pass. The way you organize and put things together is going to determine how well people receive your dream. There's no way you can have a million-dollar dream with a two-dollar package. This is not to say that you need to have a ton of money, but what you do spend on your dream must be well worth it. I am always someone who is big on quality; if something does not look good to me, I just won't buy it. It is very true that a book is judged by its cover, so your dream needs to be wrapped with the best of the best. It needs to hold the standard of a professional image at all times.

When it comes to your dream you cannot afford to settle for less than what you first envisioned. If you do this you can lose sight of your original vision without understanding that it was the original vision that kept you excited in the first place. My point is that the packaging of your dream has to be equal to, or higher than your original vision. If you don't feel you have what it takes to complete the formatting of your dream, than you must connect with someone who is able to help you. While formatting and presentation can sometimes be a difficult thing to do, you must not lose sight that when it's all said and done, you will have a finished product and you will realize that it was all worth it.

6. Marketing and Networking

You are required to explore every possible marketing opportunity out there that will help you in fulfilling your dream. This includes marketing materials, classes and seminars. Whatever steps that is necessary to give you the proper marketing platform is what you need to explore. This is also a big deal when it comes to bringing your dreams to pass, because it requires diligence and discipline. The more people that know about your dream, means the more people that are likely to invest in your dream. The goal is to get as many people on board as possible, so don't be afraid to let people know about your dream. The amount of marketing that you do will always be the testimony to your efforts that bring this dream to pass. You must have a business mentality in order to see this happen. When I worked for an insurance company they were very big on marketing and networking. They stressed that no matter how many times you receive a 'no' it gets you closer and closer to your 'yes'. But you have to market! Market! Market!

Marketing and networking may cost you time and money, but is extremely necessary for you to pay now and eat later. Your marketing and networking is going to serve as the miles per hour for your dream. The speed or pace of your dream will be determined by the amount of consistent marketing you do.

Furthermore, people are interested in new dreams and ideas. You must keep in mind that somebody is waiting to hear about your dream, and you must not allow yourself to get into the mindset of excusing marketing and networking because you feel like your dream is unworthy. The wonderful thing about us is that without each other, we cannot go higher. We all need each other, and a smart business professional understands the power of marketing and networking. They understand that there may be someone out there who can perfect my dream which just might benefit the both of us. Keep in mind that there is always someone who has a piece to your puzzle, and the only way to find that is through network and marketing.

It's easy to feel like your dream is unimportant when you go to events and you see people with easier solutions. You can slip into believing that your dream means nothing amongst other dreamers. Some dreams have a greater demand on them, but it doesn't mean that one is better than the other. If you have a dream of creating a custom Popsicle company in your city, but your companion has a dream of opening a children's hospital, you must not get discouraged in believing that your dream is stupid. Remember, your dream is the daughter of your purpose. That Popsicle Company might lead to a Popsicle factory and recreation center where kids can come and create as many custom popsicles as they desire. It may just so happen to sit right across the street from the hospital, which houses the children with cancer. This Popsicle factory may be the only place within walking distance for these kids to get away and enjoy themselves.

Never discredit the power of your dream. There is no such thing as a stupid dream, and there is no such thing as a more important dream. Whatever you do, do not be afraid to market and network, because remember, your level of confidence in your dream will determine the level of confidence that others have in your dream. Don't worry about how it appears to haters because if it was left up to them, you wouldn't have had a dream to begin with. True entrepreneurs would never discredit or look down upon another entrepreneur. With knowing how hard it is to get past your feelings long enough to achieve your dreams, you should have a level of compassion and respect for anyone else that is working hard to pursue their dream. Dreamers respect other dreamers, especially when they know what it takes to bring a dream to pass.

Make sure your other steps are finished and you have a completed product or project before you begin to network and market. I was talking to my friend about her business that she desired to start. She wanted to open up a beauty supply store so I explained to her that she must ensure that she has a completed project before she starts to advertise and market. Reason being, is because not everything will go as we plan, so the first time something comes up we will start to feel like we did not do a good job on everything.

Someone can come in and say mean things such as "This hair is not quality hair; you need to shut this store down because it's a rip off." I told her that when this happens, she will not be discouraged because she will remember that she researched the quality of every piece that entered her store. Instead of feeling like she did not do a good job at selecting her products, she will not be offended but instead, she will recognize that this customer does not know quality. For this reason make sure that you complete all of your steps before advertising, marketing, and networking.

7. Discipline and Consistency
This is a step which sounds simple and easy to commit to, but this is the one of the hardest things to actually do. Some of us have completed great projects, but because we lacked discipline and consistency, those projects were pushed aside. Many of us don't want to accept

the fact that things don't happen for us because of our lack of consistency. Some investors will not support you just based on the fact that you have a great product or business alone; they want to see your consistency, they want to see if you have stood the test of time, and they want to know how long you've been at this thing because your consistency shows them how serious you are.

Perseverance is everything when it comes to completing any tasks whether it's school, work or starting your own business. Your determination, drive and commitment to your dream despite of any opposition are all necessary for making it to the finish line.

8. Stay Focused

Your dream must have most of your undivided attention so that you can ensure that it's completed to your expectation. In order to achieve this, you must stay focused because your dream depends on it. When you are in the process of working on your dream, you don't have much room to play around. If you feel your dream burning within you, there will be very few things that should be able to throw you off. Stick to the plan and let nothing take you off course. Some people will try to get you to abort your dream by sucking you in to their drama-filled lives which can make you emotional. While you are walking out, your dream you cannot let your emotions dictate your progress.

All sorts of things will try to distract you such as relationships, family issues, financial issues and more. Move past how you feel, and I'm telling you that when this happens you will feel like a conqueror, not just because you completed something, but because you had enough determination to move past your emotional-self. A person who is able to conquer their own emotions is one who is unstoppable.

9. Set a Deadline

Every dream should have an appropriate deadline. If your dream is important, you will most definitely set the most appropriate deadline for it. This deadline must not be too far that you have room to slack off, and it must not be too close to where it can discourage you if it doesn't happen. Take into consideration others who have completed the same dream, do your research and try to find a reasonable deadline for it. Understand that your dream could be completed in phases, so there may be more than one deadline that needs to be set. A deadline gives you accountability to your dream and makes certain that you have very little room for distraction.

Believe it or not, people are more receptive when you tell them that you can't hang out because you have to meet a deadline, as opposed to telling them that you're working on a project. For some reason, people would rather be rejected with your deadline then your honest desire to want to reach your dreams. They may say something like 'I have dreams too, but you don't see me neglecting my friends and family.' This is to get you to miss your deadline. If they are truly your supporters, they will not make you compromise your dream. Instead, they will want you to not only work towards it, but actually achieve your dream on time.

You must set a deadline and stick to it because your dream is most dependent upon one. Make it your priority to reject any form of guilt so that you can effectively work on your dream. When it's all over with, your people will be proud of you and you will be satisfied with yourself. Once you have achieved one dream, there is no turning back and you should have strong confidence that the other dreams are but a thought away from coming to pass.

Every day we should be doing something to achieve our goals. When you set out on the journey to fulfill your dream, you must commit yourself to doing something that gets you one step closer to making that dream a reality. The truth of the matter is that so many things will demand your immediate attention and your dream will be the first thing pushed to the side. All of us have major responsibilities that require us to give our full undivided attention, and this is very understandable. For this reason, each day should be dedicated to completing something that helps you fulfill your dream.

It's funny how many of us can be more dedicated and committed to another person's dream, but when it comes to our own we are relaxed and nonchalant about it. We see our dream as something we don't have to do, as something that can wait. Some of us know we need to go back to school complete our degree so that we can land that dream job. For whatever reason, it is looked at like more of a task done on our leisure time such as a hobby rather than a required responsibility essential for our livelihood. I do not discriminate against people who are content with not doing anything to complete their dream; I am speaking to those who want it with a passion, and desire clear direction on how to achieve it. My efforts in encouraging are only to provoke the inner motivation that you possess for fulfilling your dream. I want to see as many people succeed in life as possible.

When I look around, I see the signs of the end times approaching, we should all be fulfilling our dream before Jesus gets back. God gave us this land and placed us here to enjoy ourselves and to have fun, so why not fulfill our dream before Jesus comes back in town? I want to help you achieve your dream this year. The first thing I'm charging you to do is to draw closer to God through the Lord Jesus Christ, so that you can see the fullness of what God has for you. Second thing I'm charging you to do is to start taking aggressive steps in fulfilling your dream so that you can be complete, knowing that you are fulfilling your purpose in life. Notice that the main person who benefits from these two things is you. If you start your journey to fulfilling these two things, you will begin to feel whole.

Peace in Your Mind

As you are fulfilling your dream make sure that you maintain your stress levels, because every day is not going to be easy, but you will get through easier if you understand how to maintain a peaceful mind. Many people quit their dream even though things are going well and life is really good. One of the reasons why this happens is because of the inability to handle the stress that came with the dream that they had.

Sister Brother Talk

I went home to Sandusky Ohio one weekend to visit my family, and I was speaking to my older brother. I was telling him about the book and the ministry that God has given me, and he started to give me some really good advice. He told me to make sure that everything is in order before I expose my dream to the world. He was explaining to me that the current year would be the year in which the foundation is laid. He encouraged me to commit myself to making 2015 the year of preparation, then 2016 would most definitely be the year of exposure. He told me to get everything in order and get ready to fire one bullet after the next so that I can go forward with an unstoppable force.

I admired this advice from him because I can easily see that when everything is not completed prior to launching whether it is exposing our dream to the world, or starting a business, it can be more difficult and discouraging to finish. People want to know that you have a well thought out idea and if your plan is bulletproof. Until you get everything together, you give people nothing. Set your deadline and give nothing until you meet that deadline.

Dream Accountability Partner

Many of us have our dream mapped out and some of us have already exceeded these steps. An accountability partner is very much needed for anyone who is fulfilling their dream. When I first began writing this book, I expressed it to a few people and everyone seemed very happy for me, but there was one person in particular who was holding me accountable to my dream. I will forever be grateful for my friend Tatiana for her sacrifice and support of me completing this book. We would talk every day about business and how the book was coming along. It was so amazing to have someone who viewed the light of my dream like I did. It was like every time I made progress I had someone to share the news with.

Even as God would give me different revelations for the book, she would ask me "what has God shown you today, how far have you come?" And every time I would give her my progress, her response was always "I'm so excited." This is what made writing the book so much fun, because I had a dream accountability partner who was experiencing the writing of the book with me.

Be sure to find an accountability partner who is just as excited as you are. The accountability partner that you choose must also have a dream that they are pursuing. The relationship is not healthy when it's one-sided because the accountability partner may feel used after a while. It's very important for you to support that person as well. If you are holding them accountable, and they are holding you accountable then no one can be selfish in believing that their dream is more important than the others. I suggest you only have one accountability partner, because if there is more than one, the attention could eventually go from the dreams that you all want to fulfill, to trying to balance the relationship. If you're holding another person accountable for their dream along with yourself on top of the third party, it could possibly rob you of focusing more on your dream.

Chapter 9

Speak and pray over your dream

The power of words

Some of us have faith to attempt our dreams but no faith to pray over them.

Proverbs 18:21 reminds us that *"Life and Death are in the power of the tongue and those who love it will eat its fruits."*

Our words carry power and authority, whatever you speak is exactly what you'll get. You have it within your power to make your dream as big as you want it to be. You also have it within your power to kill your dream from the root. When you speak positively in general, you position yourself to receive positive things.

Galatians 6:7 says "Do not be deceived; God is not mocked: for whatever a man sews, that he will also reap."

Whatever words you decide to speak into the atmosphere will eventually come back to you in the same frequency in which you sent them. God explains to us that this is how his words work for him.

Isaiah 55:11 *says "so shall my word be that goes forth from my mouth; it shall not return to me void, but it shall accomplish that which I sent it, and it shall prosper in the thing which I sent it."*

This lets us know that God has the ability to speak, and whatever He speaks must come to pass. We know that we are made in the image and likeness of God our father, so if he speaks something and it happens we can also do the same. Don't be afraid to say what you want your dream to look like, as long as you believe it will happen just as you say it.

It's very hard for me to surround myself with people who speak negatively about themselves or other people. When people start to say things like 'It will never happen for me and I'm not good enough, or that's just a fantasy,' those are the exact words that will come back to bite them. This is why our words should always be words of life. I challenge you to start speaking positive things about your dream, and you will not be disappointed as those positive words will begin to come back to you over time.

The power of prayer

One thing that I was always raised to do was to pray. As a little girl, if something was hurting like my stomach or my head, my great aunt, would always lay her hands on me and pray. Soon after her prayer I would feel the pain leaving my body. I really didn't understand how it worked, but I knew if I asked her to pray for me then my pain would leave. Prayer can truly be the thing that expedites your dream.

Mark 11:24 tells us *"Therefore I say to you, whatsoever things you asks when you pray, believe that you receive them, and you will have them."*

This scripture suggests that prayer is the answer. Not only prayer, but believing that after you prayed it shall come to pass. Sometimes we can get into the habit of praying and not believing our own prayers. This is why some things can't happen because the Bible says:

Hebrews 11:6. *"Without faith it is impossible to please God"*

So we know that it is not enough to just pray, it means everything when you believe. Even if it doesn't look like it's possible for your dream to come to pass keep in mind that:

2ⁿᵈ Corinthians 5:7 *"We walk by faith and not by sight"*

Understand that your vision will someday become a reality regardless of how it appears today. When you have the Lord on your side, you will always have someone cheering you along the way.

During the process of writing this book which I was determined to complete in less than 60 days, I had challenges. Most of the challenges I faced while writing the book were mainly mental challenges. I would set a goal for myself to complete a certain amount per day, and there were days that I did not feel up to it. Sometimes

I felt discouraged so it would hinder me from writing. There were days that I was just not in the mood to pull out my laptop to sit down and write as my energy levels would not allow me to, even though I knew I had to get it done.

When I would pray and read a Scripture, I would become encouraged immediately, and somehow I would receive an urgency to pick up my laptop and start writing. Before I knew it I had a chapter completed, regardless of the fact that I originally had no strength to endure it. So I'm giving you the strategies that truly helped me get through my book. Each day that I relied on God to get me through, I realize that I would look up and see that I had completed more work than I had the energy to achieve; this is the power of prayer.

Though you have challenges, physical or mental, if you rely on God and pray your way through, He is faithful to carry you on the days that you, yourself can go no longer. God would not write my book for me on the days that I did not want to write, but He gave me such a refreshing boost that was able to pick me up and carry me through to my goal for that day.

There were times when I would question whether or not I was supposed to write. I kept having these evil thoughts that would tell me my words were not powerful enough and that no one really wants to hear what I have to say. All types of thoughts were flowing through my mind telling me that I am not educated enough to write a book, that my vocabulary is not extensive enough, and if I put my book out people would see how ignorant my thoughts were. Whenever I would hear these thoughts I would begin to speak the opposite.

I would tell myself Heaven Brown is a wise woman; she is a woman of great creativity. No matter what people perceive me to be, Heaven Brown will always be known as a woman who pursued her dream. The unfortunate thing is most of us are too embarrassed to pursue our dreams; this can usually be changed by renewing your mind with the word of God or with a simple genuine prayer. If I received an objection in my mind about my education, I would immediately counteract that with a positive thought. Sometimes we blame the enemy and other people for their negativity when the reality is we have the power to shut down and counteract negativity regardless if it's coming from another person or even our very own thoughts.

I am forever changed

I remember when I first began to get closer to the Lord and I read a book that changed my life forever. This book was by Benny Hinn entitled 'Good morning Holy Spirit'. I was attending Columbus Christian centers ministry training under Dr. David C Forbes Jr. at the time. One of the requirements for the course was to read that book, and to complete a report about it. At this time, I was still unsure of whether I wanted to go and hang out and have some drinks with my friends or stay in the house to relax and pray. Some of my family and friends asked me to come home to Sandusky to have fun for the weekend. I knew that I really wanted to pursue my relationship with the Lord, but I also had a desire to go home and have fun with my friends.

I began to pray, asking God to give me strength life when suddenly I heard a knock at the door. It was the UPS man coming to deliver my brand-new book '*Good morning Holy Spirit*', which I purchased from Amazon. com. When that book arrived, I somehow knew that this was God's way of telling me to stay home. So I called my cousin and I told her that I was not coming.

As I sat there reading the words of the book I knew that my life would never be the same. Finally it felt like I was discovering who I was along with the dreams that I had as well as the calling on my life. I finished the book in just two weeks; I was so hungry for the things of God. Ever since I read that book I have not stepped foot in a club, neither have I smoked or drank alcohol. That book gave me a vivid picture of what it's like to be close to Jesus. I had no clue who Benny Hinn was, neither had I seen him before, all I knew was that his testimony changed the way I saw life and God forever. His dream was to do the will of God and his desire was to see people saved, healed and transformed by the power of the Holy Spirit.

As a 19-year-old not knowing who Benny was, I was able to watch him on YouTube and get inspired by his level of commitment to God. Who would have thought this evangelist could reach someone like me? You never know who your dream will touch, so I encourage you to just do it, and do it with obedience. I would imagine that if he would have allowed negative thoughts to prevail to the point that he stopped writing the book; I could have missed an opportunity to have a genuine relationship with the Lord. I always tell people '*Good morning Holy Spirit*' *was* one of the very first genuine encounters that

I experienced with the Lord. It was through reading that book that I received another piece of the puzzle to my purpose.

My point is that we cannot discredit our dream or listen to negative thoughts or negative people because your dream has the power to change a life. As God began to take me on the journey of fulfilling one of my desires, I started to feel a burning desire to share these things with the people around me. When I pursued the ministry that God placed within my heart, he started to birth the book. So it is my hope that you will have a life-changing experience with this book just like I did with 'Good morning Holy Spirit'. I pray that it will ignite a fire within you as you pursue your dreams. Whether you are an author or entrepreneur, someone is waiting on you and your dream.

I want my dream to have so much influence that I'm blessed and my children's children are also blessed. I always pray that my dreams go beyond my grave so that 50 and 60 years after I'm gone, my dreams can still have an effect on the generations to come.

Chapter 10

Dream connection

It's a connection issue

So many of us truly desire to go after our dreams in life and fulfill our purpose but it never happens. Sometimes we think that we are constantly making wrong turns and bad decisions. It's not even a decision-making issue, because if you're properly connected to God you will see the light shine in the way they you are supposed to go. It's a connection issue; people sometimes make bad decisions because they are not properly connected. When you have the right connection it's easy to get into the doors that God opens. Connection alone, depending on how you see it is a golden ticket into the doors that you desire to walk into. When you know the right people and you have the right connections, who can really stop you?

Connecting with God gives you the advantage when it comes to your life. Because you don't know the end from the beginning it's hard making decisions that you are unsure of. Understanding that when you go into the wrong doors God will continue to make all things work together for your good, because you love Him and are called according to His purpose.

The reality is that the average Christian is not really connected with God, they may love him and teach about him and represent him but the connection is not there. God is so good that even though the average person is not connected properly he still extends the grace that we need to make it through life. He was saying in Proverbs 16:9 go ahead and plan your way and I will direct your steps making them sure. I put that Scripture in first person so that we can understand that God's word is His point of view. This is an amazing thing that God does because it lets us know that no matter how far off we go, God who oversees us will somehow direct our path in a way that helps us to be overcome. You may not be able to live your best life because you are not properly connected, but God is so good that he leads you even though you are not connected.

People who do not believe in God will think that they are blessed because they do all sorts of things that are good that eventually come back, they call it good luck. And they also believe that the reason why terrible things happen to them is because of the terrible things that they did in the past, they call it karma. There is some truth to this form of belief, the only reason why I say that is because when you match it against the word of God you find that the concept is similar. The Bible says be not deceived God is not mocked, whatsoever a man sews that Shell he also reap.

Some of us Christians believe that our life is under the blood of Jesus and that our wrongdoings (sins) are accounted for but it is under the blood therefore any evidence of anything we have done in our past is immiscible because it is placed under the blood of Jesus. And we also understand that there spiritual forces that come and trespass into the lives of people, sometimes they are the result of bad things taking place we call it demonic activity.

And Christians also believe that the good things that happen in life are all blessings from the Creator himself, therefore the glory does not go to chance or luck but the glory goes to God, we call it divine intervention. Wouldn't it be so much easier to experience the life that God has for us in pursuing the purpose of his predestined plan if we were properly connected? If God is all-knowing (Omniscience) and we connect with him we may as well be all-knowing not because we know things on our own but because we are connected to the one who knows all in all.

Dream Connection

Dream connections are those that are necessary for everyone to win. Have you ever met a person and you realized that they are connected to you because of the dream that they have, and you're connected to them because of the dream that you have? It's a wonderful thing when you have two people who are motivated about similar things as it's not every day you get to partner with like-minded people. You may have people who understand your dream and everything that you're telling them, and they may be genuinely happy for you, but it is not the same as having someone just as motivated as you are. The blind cannot lead the blind, and it is important for your circle to be filled with people who are heading in the same direction as you.

If you don't pay close attention to the people you allow within your inner circle as you're fulfilling your dream, you will get to a place where you will have to drop them off, especially when their plan is to head down a different route. When I was around 11 years old, I created a pattern with one friend who I was very close to, she and I did everything together. It was so peaceful having that one friend simply because there was not a lot of chaos. Then, when the season was up for us, I gained another friend, and so did she. Neither one of us were angry at each other for going our separate ways.

We have to learn to recognize when our season is up for the people in our lives. Letting someone overstay their season can mean bad business for the relationship and everything involved in it. Some of us have people in our lives that we know they are no longer supposed to be there. Some of us keep them around because we are bored or because they are feeding us. This may include people who were on your dream cloud, and you may need to disconnect from them if the relationship becomes too stale.

There comes a time when we must evaluate the people who are connected to us to make sure that there is still juice flowing in the relationship. When things begin to dry out and get stale, this is when issues arise and tension increases. But keep those who have your best interest at heart, and are connected to you because of the dream you have.

What's Your Approach

When you follow your dreams knowing that people are going to receive you, that's just what is going to happen. It's all about the energy that you put out, people will respond to you based off of your energy and aura. There was a young lady who was explaining to me that she received correction about her approach and her demeanor, and when she changed this approach she began to gain friends immediately. If you want others to receive you, your approach must be receivable.

Does your dream match your personality?

When your personality matches your dream you will notice that your dream will attract the right connections. Anyone who is pursuing their dream in life must consider whether or not it matches their personality. People will become drawn to you because of your personality alone. That personality must line up with your dream, in other words your dream must be a direct reflection of your personality.

Many of us like to pursue things because others have pursued them, but if it does not match your personality, and you are not passionate for it, it will not fit your lifestyle. Under normal circumstances you will not find a boxing champion in a hair salon cutting and styling hair. It just wouldn't fit his personality, especially if he's had no prior experience or desire to open a hair salon, other than the fact that his buddy did it and is making decent money. I'm not suggesting that you should not shoot for your true desires; I am simply saying that there are parameters for personality types when it comes to fulfilling your dream. Many of us have no business trying to do something because someone else has done it.

Often times we love to do things we do not have a passion for, this is why you see people who start business after business and none of them succeed. They were a copycat rather than a creator. Be sure to check and double check your desires prior to starting your dream. This is only so you can guarantee that this dream is yours and not just yours because someone else is doing it. You will know that the dream is sincerely your own if it has been tested by time. If you have a dream at one point and that desire never left, then I would say you're probably safe. If you've had a dream and the passion is still new after a year or two this is probably something you want to take seriously enough to pursue.

When your dream starts to manifest and unfold, people will begin to give you feedback, they will start to say things like 'I always knew you would be a nurse' or 'that fits you'. If your dream fits your personality you will almost always have the ability to walk into it effortlessly. When you are doing something that you love and it fits your personality it won't be stressful in a negative way, but rather fulfilling and exciting.

Who can dream your dream for you?

Just make sure that your dream matches you, because if it doesn't people will definitely be able to see. If people notice it doesn't fit you then it won't feel right and it won't be received well by others. When I was 19, I went to a career Academy to get my (STNA) State Tested Nursing Assistant license. The reason I went for it was because as a little girl, I would always love to take care of my uncle, who had a stroke and was very sick. My grandmother noticed it right away; she began to tell me that I was a caregiver and that when I get older I would take care of people. She told me I might even be a nurse one day.

All of this was wonderful news because as a kid I thrived off of what my grandmother saw in me. Her insight meant everything, so much so that I frame my purpose from her advice. The reason is because it gave me comfort to know that what I was doing was making her proud, so her positive affirmation and feedback always encouraged me to take the advice and run with it.

As soon as I graduated high school, I began to take these classes, keep in mind my grandmother said I could do this. My mind told me that if my grandmother witnessed me as a caregiver for when I was a child, than I should have no problem getting this license and starting this career.

The major issue with this story is that this was never my dream. I don't believe that this was my grandmother's dream for my life either; it was just a simple way of acknowledging my efforts and opening my eyes to possibilities of becoming a phenomenal nurse someday. All parents and grandparents want their children to explore good careers and have a nice income someday. I genuinely believe that this was my grandmother's innocent way of encouraging me to put my skills to use someday. I went on to work in the MRDD community, before I moved to a nursing home setting. I did this work over the course of four years.

Towards the end of my career in this field, I was an activities assistant. I went throughout the nursing home helping the customers stay entertained. I would attend to their cognitive, social, and spiritual needs and sometimes their learning development. I realized that I was more effective as an Activities Assistant than I was as a nursing assistant. I liked to take care of people physically, but to do it for a living was not something I gained a lot of fun from. This is what informed me that it was never my passion to begin with.

Whenever they had new hire orientation they would explain how the nursing assistant positions should only be an option if the individual has a passion for it, and that anyone who is not passionate enough for the line of work is only likely to last a maximum of four years. It's obvious that they were right because by the end of those four years, I was burned out. I didn't want to look at another scrub uniform; neither did I want to drive passed a nursing home, the whole idea of working in the nursing home as a nursing assistant made me feel like I was a prisoner.

Another point I am trying to make is that we should never do something because other people expect us to, as the only person who will suffer the consequence is you. Make sure that your dream matches you, and is not someone else's dream for you. In my case it worked out for my good because this nursing path connected me to so many wonderful people, and I got to see the hand of God in so many ways. As we grow in life we cannot discredit the seasons of our lives that prepared us for today. I thank God for my grandmother who till this day encourages me to follow my dreams. Even for the smallest achievements she is so proud of all her children and more than happy to experience life with us.

Make a choice and go your way

When you are in the valley of decisions you will concern yourself with what door to choose. You cannot think too much about which one will be the right door. If you went through one door and bad things began to happen on that job, such as having disagreements at work or being fired: you shouldn't regret it because you never knew what dangers were behind the other door.

Even though the devil will do his worst, God will do his best; don't focus on the negative things that are coming against you as a result of the door that you chose. Be ok with your decision and Listen to your heart; understand your views and your approach to your dream, so that you can go forward with an authentic, genuine heart for fulfilling it.

If you are in the process of dating or marriage, and you are pursuing your dream or the call of God on your life, this chapter is very important for you. If you talk to other people who have been through the same circumstance they will probably tell you that your spouse can either bring life or death to your dream. Your relationship will influence your dream significantly for the good, or for the bad. My goal is to help you to understand that your partner in life is going to have a huge impact on how successful you are and everything that you do.

Women in particular struggle with having a husband who she is willing to submit to, whereas men struggle with having a wife who is willing to help him strive towards his own vision. It seems that when two people have two completely different visions for their life, they only find out after they are married and things begin to spiral downward. Here you have a man with a great call on his life, but his wife has a different dream and no plans to share her husband with the world.

Ministers, usually move around a bit. The average minister will move 8 to 10 times during their life's ministry, and sometimes more often. If you are one with the call, you will notice that your moves are continuous because of the demand of your life. Getting married, settling down and having children are one of the hardest obstacles to overcome for someone wanting to pursue their call. If this is who you are going to be, you must perfect the art of a balanced life. If you are married and have children you can relate because every houschold struggles in this area. Usually it's the children who get the most neglect.

Although I believe God's design was to see our dreams come to past, we cannot forget that He is a family man first, and neglecting the family that you created is unacceptable altogether. If your spouse has a non-portable job and you have a dream that you are pursuing for the benefit of the family that requires you to travel, understand that until you reach that level of sustainability there are sacrifices that everyone needs to be on board with. I see marriages fall apart all because somebody was not willing to make that simple sacrifice that would have positioned them for one of the best marriages that this world has ever known.

My public figure

If your dream consists of you being in the public eye continually then you really need to be selective about the husband or wife that you choose. Often time's ministers and pastors struggle with this, Celebrities are the most targeted in this area of their lives. They live in the public eye; their life is not a private matter at all. I'm sure politicians, entertainers, and celebrities can testify that people are more interested in the personal intimate details of their lives, than they are seeing them and their family happy.

Marriages don't often survive when they are constantly on display for everyone to view and criticize, and being a public figure makes it harder as you can't say "I don't want to be in the public eye any longer." It's not like a traditional job where you can call off or not show up whenever you please. Your wife can't say she doesn't feel like being around all of the attention as it doesn't work like that. Even after a divorce or separation, you are going to forever be a point of interest.

I was talking to a pastor who said that they are stressed, mainly because of the pressure placed on them, especially in their marriage. If you are a public figure or aspire to be in the public eye, understand that people are always going to look through your window even if you close the blinds. You'll have no privacy or control over your life, and you are likely to be constantly abused and misunderstood, if you do not have a suitable mate by your side, it will be very difficult to be on your dream cloud and survive. When I am having conversations with people who may be interested in me, I always ask myself within the first few seconds of conversing with them if I have a realistic picture of my life. I'm not too shallow to believe that looks are everything.

The selection process

When it comes to the dating life, I discriminate against a man by his relationship with God, the way he speaks to me and others, his energy, his looks, his age, his sense of humor as well as his education versus his experience. The reason that I am so picky is simply because I know what I want my future to look like, and I believe I'll know when I've found the right teammate to join me. It amazes me how people think they are such a victim, all because they have had more than one sour relationship or marriage.

When I see people who are divorced for their first and second times, and are unsure as to why it keeps happening to them, I tell them that the problem is down to one of two reasons, either one of them have issues, or they both have issues. If it turns out that the issue is the other person, then it is not even a matter of why these things repeat themselves, but rather their own selection in the process. God doesn't want you to be unhappy, but if you don't stop selecting the wrong people to be with, then you will continue to have this as a problem. Preparation is everything, and most marriages are too rushed, and the opportunity to properly select the right person is forfeited because of lust, infatuation, or just plain old eagerness.

Everyone chooses in their own way, but I usually try to lean on the Holy Spirit. if He says 'no' I don't get discouraged because I would rather wait and marry the right man then to suffer and marry a person that my life was never compatible with. This is one area of my life that I feel is a big deal because when you have started to achieve your dream, it can literally be destroyed by marrying the wrong person.

When you are fulfilling your dream, the enemy will send distracting connections your way to discourage you and get you off course. Problems will start to come about, causing your emotions to stir up to the point that you won't have any new ideas – Also you can get more of the responsibility such as work, family and other life issues to where your attention is no longer focused. Make sure you always stay on guard and are aware at all times. Some of them you would definitely see coming, and others may take you by surprise. Nevertheless stay on guard.

Chapter 11

On your dream cloud

This is the place where your dreams have truly come to pass. No longer are you working to accomplish your dream, but you are working to maintain it. This is where it gets a little bit easier because the hard part was getting yourself and others to truly believe in it. At this point, you are officially positioned on your dream cloud. You have silenced every naysayer and hater and no-one can deny that you are living in your dream. You've overcome the biggest objection which was you. This is a place where your train is on the move and you are going too fast to stop. People are now expecting to see your dream cloud whenever they see you. It is at this place that your dream is attached to you and this is how they know you. When people talk to you they have no choice but to ask you about your dream. Get your dream team for your dream cloud.

Not everyone is meant to join you on your dream cloud. There should be a handful of reserved spots, and only a few open opportunities. The people who have reserved spots are the ones who supported you and helped you from the beginning. I do believe if anyone these are the ones who should get special recognition along with your complete love and support just like they gave you. Most people get connected with their dream and have a tendency of forgetting the people that loved them when they were a 'nobody'. The open opportunities belong to the people who are sincere and genuine towards you and your dream. These are the ones who you picked up along the way.

I am a very introverted person and I like to be alone more than I like to be around other people, so I see it as a good thing to have as few people around you as possible. When you are on a big dream cloud sometimes people think that you are taking on recruits, so they try all types of manipulation just to get you to let them on your dream cloud. Some will attempt to make you feel bad by saying 'Don't forget where you come from.' If you are one who is currently in your dream life, I want to encourage you to not feel guilty or get discouraged and enjoy your dream cloud the way you want to.

When you are on your dream cloud you will usually be very busy, and sometimes you may not be able to hang out or talk on the phone like you used to. This is the place where your friendships will be challenged. When you were not on your dream cloud no-one got offended when you didn't call or text, but now everyone's offended as if you were that close to them to begin with. When you come to this place you must remain humble, because people are going to throw as many darts at you as they possibly can. It will usually be people who are spiteful because they don't see a way out for themselves.

When this starts to happen, it can turn you into a bitter person and start to get to your head. In other words, if you're not careful you can slip into pride and think that you have arrived because of the haters piling up on you. Some people view haters as motivation, and instead of getting discouraged they start to enjoy the attention. There has to be a balance if you want to truly enjoy yourself on your dream cloud. You must not allow people to tear you down, and you must be careful so that other people's opinions cannot make you see yourself more or less than what you are.

Not everyone belongs

When you are living the dream, not everyone should be allowed on your cloud. Truth is, just like you had people who criticized you for achieving your dreams; you will most definitely have people that will try to tell you how you should live your dream.

Usually the people who are in your life have direct access to you or indirect access to you. Just because they are part of your dream team does not mean they should be too close to you. On your dream team, you may have a graphic designer who specifically does your graphics. You don't talk to him on a daily basis but you bless him in various ways because he does a good job on your graphics. You are helping his dream and he is helping yours. He is on the business end of your dream team. You also have others on your dream team like those who are in your life on a regular basis, such as friends and family. These are the people who are not offering you anything material for your dream, but they do offer support. These people are most beneficial when they are close to you. The graphic designer is most beneficial for you from the distance.

Designated roles

Everyone on your team needs to have a definite role and if those roles are not defined, we need to know when to step in and to define them. If you have set it up for one person to be the cashier as you are selling your jewelry at your jewelry parties, it means that the cashier cannot be a food server as their role is to specifically be the cashier. Everyone on your dream team needs to understand their role and they have to also be okay with them. If you delegate a role to someone that they are not comfortable with, and then the chances are that the individual won't be a part of your dream team for long.

You may have people that take care of your children for you, and they have to be okay with that role. No-one on your dream team should feel more or less important than the other. It's obvious that the people who were with you from the beginning will be envious because of their longevity with you, but your dream team is just that - a team, so don't feel guilty especially when you know deep within yourself everyone is important including the ones who were there when you had nothing.

Time of testing

There will be times where you feel like God is not helping you, or God is not with you. Some of us may experience some financial challenges that discourage us when it comes to fulfilling our dream. I believe that there are seasons where the Lord tests our faith to see if we will give up or still believe. Everything gets tested, your dream, your relationship with God, sometimes even your relationship with other people. But in these testing's you'll find that the testing is only to reveal what's on the inside of you.

When we go to school we have exams that were usually set up to test everything that we've learned. The test is not there to embarrass you or make you look bad, but rather to praise you for all of your hard work. At the end of every test you will receive a reward according to your performance. The thing about a test is that no-one can do it for you and no-one should be helping you. The test is to prove your diligence all this time. Getting discouraged because you are in a testing season is not acceptable as you are only being tested for your own benefit. God is a just God and he will not test you in an area that he has not yet taught you. If you are getting tested for something, please understand that you have already been equipped for it.

I recall going through a time of testing with a company that I worked for. It was a very stressful and discouraging situation, I absolutely dreaded going to work every day and I remember often going out to my car to pray. This work situation was far from the vision that I saw for myself, and I knew that this was not what God had planned for me. I wanted to give up and quit so that I wouldn't have to bother myself with the job anymore. As I began to cry out to God, he started to lead me to finish out my assignment at that place. He said "I need you to not quit this job, but stick it out and you will see that the result is better than the process." He also gave me a Scripture:

Matthew 23:12 and said *"and who ever exalts himself will be humbled, and he who humbles himself will be exalted."*

I stood on this scripture day and night when I was going through hell at that job. What I didn't understand was that God was setting me up for a breakthrough. They eventually let me go and finally the torture was over. If felt so good to finally be free from that employer. After this, I was able to not work a traditional job for eight months.

It was during the eight months that God began to give me business ideas, ministry assignments and speaking engagements. Sixty of those days were spent writing this book. When I look back at the testing, I realize that God was putting my character on display before my very eyes and also for people to see. I learned that the testing was a set up for the awesome blessing thereafter. If I would have quit, the cards would have played out a little different. During that time God blessed me with a big check that held me for my expenses until I completed everything that I was supposed to.

My desire is to not work for man, I realize that I am determined to have multiple streams of income that do not require me to punch a clock for someone else. My desire is to provide opportunities for others to fulfill their dream. So that time of testing brought out things that were in me that I never even knew existed. This is usually what God does to elevate us. He will sometimes send a storm to help secure us in our next level. When you get promoted in a position, it's usually because you have proved yourself worthy for the title. I'm here to tell you not to get discouraged in your season of testing as it just means that God has an amazing reward for your diligence. If you are able to endure the trials and tests coming against you right now, I guarantee you God will exalt you when it's all said and done.

> **Hebrews 12:11 "no discipline seems pleasant at the time, but painful. Later on, however, it produces a harvest of righteousness for those who have been trained by it."**

For many of us, the test that we feel the most is in the financial sense, but God is faithful to those who keep his word.

> **Matthew 6:26 says "look at the birds of the air; they do not so or read, neither do they reap, nor do they gather in their barn, and yet your heavenly father feeds them. Are you not worth much more than they?"**

You and I are the highest form of creation; you are the unique expression of God, so if he can provide for the birds of the sky then surely he can provide for you. When I look into the depth of the Scripture, it sounds like God is trying to convey to us that the birds do not earn anything to get God's help, neither are we required to earn help from God. If you never put a dime in church or do another good deed, God will still take care of you, He is just that gracious.

God did it for me

Before approaching your dream you must know that you will be tested by fire so that while you are on your dream cloud you can easily withstand any attack heading your way. I remember when I was about 22; I had been in Ohio for three years at that time and had very little help from anyone, as I was very much an independent person. During the course of that year I fell on hard times and I had no idea how I was going to get out from the mess I created for myself.

I was very discouraged because I had nowhere to live, no job and no money, but here I was professing to be a worker in the kingdom of God. My credit was completely messed up, I owed multiple management companies for apartments that I previously had. No-one was willing to give me an opportunity; every time I applied for an apartment I was denied. Everyone who has ever lived in apartment communities knows that when you apply for an apartment the two things that they are concerned about are your current employment status and your credit score. I had neither one at my disposal. This means I was doomed before I even tried. I was living with a lady and I had overstayed my welcome, so it was time for me to go.

My family didn't know this at the time, but there were days that I was sleeping in the car with most of my belongings in the truck. I remember praying and asking God to get me through my current situation. It just didn't seem right to me because there I was, a servant of the most high God I loved him with all of my heart, I was going to church, and paying I tithes and doing all that I knew, yet here I was homeless and discouraged.

131

I was thinking how it could happen to me out of all people; I could understand if I was a participating sinner of this would, as it make sense. I was in a self-righteous state of mind and the only way for me to get out of that situation was to humble myself, and accept the work that God was doing for me. Even though those were some hard days, somehow I knew God was going to bring me out. One day as I was praying I asked the Lord what I was supposed to do to get myself out of the situation. I heard him say that when you get up on Monday morning, the first apartment community that you step your foot in will be yours.

So when Monday morning came around I went to an apartment community that I thought was really nice. When I applied for the apartment I explained to the leasing consultant that I owed to other apartments from my past living situation. I also explained to her that I had very little money and no job. Most apartment communities would have looked at me and asked 'How could you possibly come in here requesting an apartment that you don't deserve, one that you can't afford currently with no job to pay for it in the future'. Clearly I was insane, but I knew that God was with me the whole time, even if she wanted to say no – she couldn't.

When God says yes, what man can say no? When God says no, what man can say yes? The lady looked at me like I was crazy and the words that came from her mouth were "Don't worry, we will figure it out." I took those as the words of God and I began to feel love and care for Him all over again. After completing the application process, I left so that she could do the screening necessary for approval. That same day the lady called me and explained that indeed I was not qualified for the apartment, but the next words that I heard from her mouth was "you are conditionally approved." She told me to get a statement notarize saying that I would eventually pay off the debt that I owed to the previous community. She told me that if I could fulfill that request then she would approve me. When I went back to pick up my key and sign my lease, I noticed the maintenance man working in the office looked at me and asked if I needed help moving everything. I told him I needed help and that I had only a few hours to get everything moved.

That day was so encouraging because not only did I get the apartment that God promised me, but I never had to lift a finger. The maintenance guys moved all of my belongings in just two hours. Before I knew it, I looked around and I realized that God had done it for me. I was so amazed at how he moved on my behalf and worked it all out for my good. As I look back on this test and trial that I endured I realize that this was building my faith muscles. Now, if I ever find myself in this situation again where I hit rock bottom, I know without a shadow of a doubt that God's going to see me through and nothing will be impossible for me. Keep in mind that God can and will take care of your every need no matter what it is, just trust that He is with you especially when you are on your dream cloud.

Burning Bridges on your dream cloud

As human beings, we are naturally confrontational in some way. Even if you are not a confrontational person there's always someone who has the ability to press your buttons. So this is a very important chapter for those who do not welcome confrontation in their lives on purpose. It's very easy for a business deal to go sour even without that being your intention. When you are on your dream, you will experience your share of jealous people. For this reason you must not give in to any drama that will conflict with business or your dream cloud.

On the other hand, begin to follow your dream and God will start to send you many bridges that connect you to wherever it is that you need to go next. These bridges will come in the form of human beings not understanding that they are sent by God to give you the missing piece of your dream puzzle. If you are not careful, you will miss these opportunities when they arise for you. It's easy to be intimidated or closed-minded when God starts to send these resources. I recall speaking to my friend one day about her business. We talked about how she could get started in public speaking as well as getting businesses to request her services. Less than two minutes later, God gives her what she asked for.

I went into class that night and I was talking to her by phone at the same time that I was walking in the door. There was a lady in the room seated with a few other women who were working on some business solutions. I was conversing with her about how I could connect with her on a business level and she asked me to give her a little bit about my background, so I explained a few things that I do on the business end, along with my work experience, and she in a matter of two minutes gave me three different resources that would enhance the platform of not only my business, but also my friends.

My friend and I were looking for opportunities to get business from other people, but after speaking to this woman she gave us resources that would help business come to us. This is how God works when it comes to fulfilling your dream. As you go God will go with you, He'll start to give you the pieces of the puzzle that you need to get you to the next place for your dream. On a personal observation, I picked up quite a bit of confidence from this woman as we were speaking, along with a strong competitive and assertive personality. This woman appeared to me as a business woman and her demeanor expressed that she does not play around.

It could have easily been taken the wrong way and I could have assumed that this woman was very arrogant and prideful. But I chose to look at her as a woman who had something that I needed. She offered me to have coffee with her so that we could discuss further details about how I could be a part of her business ventures. The point I am trying to make is that this woman had a very standoffish attitude, but the approach that I came with eventually allowed her to open the door and give me the information that I was looking for. I would have never gotten that far with her if I had been offended by her demeanor.

I can easily see how her demeanor could have caused me to burn that bridge before it even began. Usually a proud and arrogant demeanor expresses to other people that they are above you. I did not allow her demeanor to hinder me from receiving what I needed from her. Her demeanor said 'little girl what do you want?' But my demeanor said 'You have something I want, and I'm not afraid of you'. I explained to this lady that I have a sales mentality to which she said I already know because you worked your way from the front of the room to the back of the room without my permission and I could say nothing to you. I want you to see how you cannot allow confrontation, or personal views to interfere with your dream. The last thing you want to do is burn bridges before you get a chance to cross them. Be open to the opportunities that God sends your way so that you can receive every piece of the puzzle that is due to you.

Give back

When you are on your dream cloud it is very important that you keep a mind of humility. We should constantly find ways to give back to others. Your dream cloud is the place where you have achieved your goal and things are looking well. This is the place where you cannot forget about the people who helped you get there along with the community of upcoming dreamers. You should not want to give back just so you can look good in front of people, it has to be a genuine desire to see other people achieve their dreams as well.

This is very important because your giving back should not have a selfish motive behind it, neither to be seen or for exposure, but for the depth of your heart. People need to know that you still care about others, and that it doesn't change just because you are on your dream cloud.

Pursuing one dream is just the beginning of fulfilling your purpose. God has so many things in store for you and when you tap into your dreams, you will see your life will increase. Delight yourself in God and listen to his leading and you will be more successful than you ever thought you could. Start listening to yourself also; you will be surprised that many of the deep answers you seek are already right there inside of you. Take your dream journey seriously; it will have a huge impact in your life. Your dream journey will unravel the dreams that have been in you. Do not be afraid to challenge yourself and do some soul searching, these are the keys that can take you to your next level, but you must first figure out what has been a hindrance. I'm excited about your new journey and most importantly your *dream journey.* God bless you.

Farewell

Thank you so much for reading this book. My prayer is that you were encouraged and motivated to pursue your dreams. If you have already started I pray that this book helped put things into perspective for you to take it to another level. I approached this book from a different angle than most. My heart kept telling me to be sure to mention the hindrances so that people can be aware of them. Most of us have things that have hindered us for years such as fear, distractions, social media, negative connections and even jealousy. We are often unable to get to the root issue, so my intention was to expose the hindrances and to uproot them so that the dreamer can move forward freely. I was always told that you cannot move forward with your future until you first deal with your past. Please do not cheat yourself; I encourage you to take that journey of searching out why your dream hasn't happened yet.

If there is no-one willing to rejoice with you, know that God had you in mind for this and I am the one person who is excited with you. If this book has truly inspired you to pursue your dream, then don't hesitate to tell me about it. You can connect with me by visiting my website at www.heavenbrown.com

I want to hear from you as soon as possible.

Heaven Brown

Prayer

I ask that you pray so that you are including God in on your plans. He will in turn reveal to you His plans for your dream and ultimately your purpose. Go ahead and pray this prayer with me and I believe that God will began to speak to you concerning your dreams along with his plan for your life.

Heavenly father I thank you for the plan you have for my life. Your word says that you know the plans you have for me, plans to prosper me and not to harm me, plans to give me hope and an expected end. Right now I surrender to those plans and my prayer is that you will lead and guide me along the way. You said that if I plan my way that you would direct my steps. I'm grateful that you have given me a desire to begin my dreams and now I am certain that the desires of my heart are in the will of God because I delight myself in you. Lord please reveal to me any areas of my life that are hindering me from achieving my dreams and going to the next level that you have already called me to. Give me the wisdom and the strength to overcome and change everything that is within my power. I believe that you are my strength and through the power of the Holy Spirit you will keep my flame kindled for the dream that is within me. From this day forward I will not try to go ahead of you, I will not try to figure out my whole purpose. I will take one day at a time and mastered the art of being a good steward over the knowledge and the pieces that you have entrusted to me. From this day on I will see my dreams as your dreams my plans as your plans my focus is to remain in sync with you. So Lord I give you permission to use my arms use my feet use my hand use my mouth use my eyes and use my mind to fulfill your purpose for my life. My agenda is your agenda so my prayer is that you will continue to bless me as I go forward in Jesus name. Enlarge my territory as I fulfill my dreams so that you can use me for your glory. In the name of the Lord Jesus I pray Amen!

Dream journey

This short assessment is to help you define what your dream is and how you will achieve it. It will also help you to understand what has been hindering you thus far and how you can overcome those objections.

Chapter 1

1. What is your dream?

_____

_____

_____

_____

2. Do you believe that you are good enough wise enough and driven enough to pursue your dream? Why or why not?

_____

_____

_____

_____

_____

3. If you are being hindered in some way shape or form what is in the way of you pursuing your dream?

_____

_____

_____

_____

_____

4. Would it be stepping too far out of your comfort zone to pursue your dream? Why or why not?

_____

_____

_____

_____

5. When do you think is the best time to start?

_____

_____

_____

_____

_____

6. When you start pursuing your dream, can you dedicate yourself to giving it your all? If so how will you do so?

_____

_____

_____

_____

_____

7. If you have already started your dream, are you motivated enough to see it finished?

_____

_____

_____

_____

8. Who and or what motivates you to work toward your dream.

_____

_____

_____

_____

_____

9.   God has given us the power to create our own world, do you feel as though you created your world to your liking thus far.

_____

_____

_____

_____

_____

10. Understanding that we first came from the imagination of God, use your imagination and write down every idea that comes to mind concerning your dream, and be creative.

_____

_____

_____

_____

_____

Chapter 2

1. Do you feel like your purposeless? Why or why not?

    _____

    _____

    _____

    _____

2. Do you have any ideas about what your purpose is in life? If so describe.

    _____

    _____

    _____

    _____

3. Take 365, times it by your age (365 x age). What is the number of days you have been on this earth?

    _____

    _____

    _____

_____

_____

4. Take the number of your days and minus 6570, which is the first 18 years of your life (days-6570). What is the number of adult days that you have had the freedom to explore life and pursue your dream?

_____

_____

_____

_____

_____

5. Understanding that your days are numbered and tomorrow is not promised, are you ready to finally start the clock on fulfilling your purpose?

_____

_____

_____

_____

_____

6. Are you aware that God is leading you as you pursue your dream and your life's purpose?

_____

_____

_____

_____

_____

7. Knowing that God does not choose how you spend your days but he knows how you should spin them. Can you commit yourself to daily prayer and devotion so that you can ensure that you are on the right path every day?

_____

_____

_____

_____

_____

8. Usually when God shows us our purpose he shows us in part, do you feel like you have enough pieces of the puzzle to get you started? If not what do you feel you're missing?

_____

_____

_____

_____

_____

9. Do you feel the call to ministry? If so what are you called to do within the ministry?

_____

_____

_____

_____

_____

10. If you are already in ministry, do you feel you are purposed to do other things outside of the ministry? If so please describe.

_____

_____

_____

_____

_____

11. When it's all over and you get to me got on that day, will you be proud of how you spent your days? Why or why not?

_____

_____

_____

_____

_____

Chapter 3

1. Do you feel like fear has been in the way of you fulfilling your dream? And if so what have you been fearful of.

_____

_____

_____

_____

_____

2. Do you fear that people will judge you? If so what gave you this indication?

_____

_____

_____

_____

_____

3. Have you ever attempted to pursue your dream
    but you didn't have the courage? If so what stole
    your determination?

_____

_____

_____

_____

_____

4. Knowing that what you choose to do with your
    dreams affect your family's future, what steps
    will you take to overcome this enemy called fear?

_____

_____

_____

_____

_____

5. When you feel fearful do you have anyone to express yourself to? I would suggest that you start talking to God about your feelings and rebuke fear every time you feel it. Write down some of the concerns you want God to know concerning the fear and ask Him to remove it.

_____

_____

_____

_____

_____

6. What grudges if any are you holding onto? Create an action plan for forgiveness because grudges can hinder some of your biggest blessings. Forgiveness also brings freedom.

_____

_____

_____

_____

_____

7. What insecurities do you have about yourself?

_____

_____

_____

_____

_____

8.   What insecurities do you have about your dream?

_____

_____

_____

_____

_____

9.   For what reason are you afraid to be yourself at times?

_____

_____

_____

_____

_____

10. Do you feel like people have placed you in their box? If so what will you do to come out and be free to express yourself and your dreams?

_____

_____

_____

_____

_____

Chapter 4

1. Can you remember one of the very first times that you experienced rejection and how it devastated you?

_____

_____

_____

_____

_____

2. Explain how you handle rejection and what you do to protect yourself.

_____

_____

_____

_____

_____

3. Do you feel like experiencing rejection has made you less confident as a person so much that you question not only your dream but your ability to make good decisions? If so in what ways has it affected you?

_____

_____

_____

_____

4. If being yourself and following your dreams can sometimes get you rejected, do you feel like you've become a different person? If so are you're ok with the way you've developed as a result.

_____

_____

_____

_____

_____

5. Do you feel like you are a torn person who sometimes can't decide on anything? If so, give an example.

_____

_____

_____

_____

_____

6. Does validation from others give you a sense of security about yourself?

_____

_____

_____

_____

_____

7. If validation is a serious issue for you in what ways do you seek it?

_____

_____

_____

_____

_____

8. Do you feel like you're constantly trying to overcompensate for your fear of rejection with the way your dress or the way that you speak? If so in what ways?

_____

_____

_____

_____

_____

9. Do you feel like your personality as a whole conflicts with others too much so you impersonate someone that you're not just so they won't reject the real you?

_____

_____

_____

_____

_____

10. Do you feel like your environment and your current situation in life provokes you to feel rejected at times, thus causing you to not follow your dream. If so in what ways?

_____

_____

_____

_____

_____

11. If your fear of rejection is hindering your dream, what steps do you feel is necessary so that this will no longer be an issue?

_____

_____

_____

_____

_____

12. Because self- awareness helps you feel more confident about what you have to offer the world, can you commit to be conscience about your feelings especially in those moments where you feel rejected, and can you learn to effectively communicate these things to the Lord and someone you truly trust.

_____

_____

_____

_____

_____

Chapter 5

1. Everyone has things that they are ashamed of, is there something in particular about your life that causes you to feel more shame than usual?

_____

_____

_____

_____

_____

2. When you feel shameful, do you feel like hiding is the best way to protect yourself?

_____

_____

_____

_____

_____

3. When you feel broken and shameful, do you have a safe place to go where you can go, and people accept you for the good bad and the ugly that you bring to the table, if so where and in what ways do you feel comfort around them? What commonality do you have if any?

_____

_____

_____

_____

_____

4. According to the Scripture in first John 19 confession ushers in forgiveness and cleansing. Can you confessed your wrongs so that you can be free from shame?

_____

_____

_____

_____

_____

5. Do you feel you have too much to lose which is why you are not open about the things that make you shameful? If so do you think you will ever get to a place of true honesty where you are not afraid of exposing your nakedness to others? If not please expound as to why it will never happen.

_____

_____

_____

_____

_____

6. Are you aware that God is with you and cares about your feelings as well as your Shame? If so in what ways do you know this?

_____

_____

_____

_____

_____

7. Do you feel like you're afraid to pursue your dreams because of your fear of failing? What are some areas pertaining to your dream that you're afraid you will fail at?

_____

_____

_____

_____

_____

8. Do you feel like you are currently a failure in life? If so why do you feel this way?

_____

_____

_____

_____

_____

9. Has anyone ever expressed to you that you will never amount to anything in life? If so who was this person and have you forgiven them?

_____

_____

_____

_____

_____

10. When you see a person who has accomplished more than you at your age do you ever feel inferior to them, like you will never achieve what they have?

_____

_____

_____

_____

_____

11. Naturally we all have a tendency to compare ourselves with others; this can sometimes send us in a fearful state especially if we become inferior. In what ways would you commit yourself to being okay with where you are, and in what ways will you strive to be where you want to be?

_____

_____

_____

_____

_____

12. Understanding that dreams are allergic to the fear of failure, what do you think is the best way for you to overcome the fear failure?

_____

_____

_____

_____

_____

Chapter 6

1. Knowing them being a dreamer can mean war, are you willing to go against what people want for you even if it means you have to fight for what you desire to do. If so how will you begin this journey?

_____

_____

_____

_____

_____

2. Do you often feel rebuked when you share details about your dream? If so why do think they rebuke you?

_____

_____

_____

_____

_____

3. In what ways are you prepared to battle the opposing forces for your dream.

_____

_____

_____

_____

_____

4. Have you allowed others to dictate your dream
    and how you should go about it? Please describe

_____

_____

_____

_____

_____

5. Do you have a circle of people who are intimidated
    by your dream? If so why do you think they
    are intimidated by you and are you approaching
    your dream in a way that welcomes Jealousy? If
    not how do you handle them?

_____

_____

_____

_____

_____

6. Do you have someone who supports and holds you accountable for your dream? IF so what ways do they help you?

_____

_____

_____

_____

_____

7. When you tell those around you about your plans for your future endeavors do you feel like they are excited for you? Why or why not

_____

_____

_____

_____

_____

8. If no one supports your dream from this day on do you feel you can remain focused and encouraged enough to pursue it anyway? Why or why not

_____

_____

_____

_____

_____

9. What distractions do you currently have in your life right now that is hindering you from pursuing or fulfilling your dream?

_____

_____

_____

_____

_____

10. Do you feel like your spouse is supportive of your dream? If not why do you think this is?

_____

_____

_____

_____

_____

11. Do you see areas in which your pursuit of your dream can have a detrimental effect on your marriage and or your family, or be too risky? If so name the things that will affect your family.

_____

_____

_____

_____

_____

12. List a few things it would take to get your spouse on board with your dream and why you think this would get your spouse to change their mind.

_____

_____

_____

_____

_____

Chapter 7

1. Do you currently have social media accounts? Why or why not?

_____

_____

_____

_____

_____

2. What are your reservations about social media? How do you think social media can distract you from your dream?

_____

_____

_____

_____

3. Is connecting with others on social media important to you why or why not?

_____

_____

_____

_____

_____

4. How do you feel social media can benefit you, and help you fulfill your dream?

_____

_____

_____

_____

_____

5. Are you tempted to use social media as a place to go vent? Where do you weigh in on the issue of using social media as an outlet?

_____

_____

_____

_____

_____

6. For you personally do you feel having social media accounts are crucial to your dream in this season of your life? If so what steps will you do to take your dream to the next level using social media?

_____

_____

_____

_____

_____

7. IF you have social media accounts currently in place do you use them as a personal platform or a professional platform.

_____

_____

_____

_____

_____

8. Do you feel you do a good job of being mindful of your post on social media? If so in what ways are you conscience of this.

_____

_____

_____

_____

_____

9. Do you know of anyone who has been a victim of cyber bullying while trying to use social media on a personal or professional platform? If so explain how this affected the life and the destiny of the victim.

_____

_____

_____

_____

_____

10. If you were ever in a situation where someone was cyber stalking or cyber bullying you through social media how would you handle it? Would you continue to pursue your dream in the public eye if your dream depends on it?

_____

_____

_____

_____

_____

11. Are you addicted to social media so much that it is affecting your ability to actively work towards your dream. If so please explain how you got to that point and how you plan to discipline yourself?

_____

_____

_____

_____

_____

12. Can you commit to using social media responsibly and ensuring that you will use it to your advantage to pursue your dream?

_____

_____

_____

_____

_____

Chapter 8

1. Do you feel like your dream is worth pursuing? Why or why not?

_____

_____

_____

_____

_____

2. Are you aware of how to execute your dream? If so list some things that it will take to complete your dream.

_____

_____

_____

_____

_____

3. Cast your vision for your dream, write down where you see your dream and describe in detail what it looks like.

_____

_____

_____

_____

_____

4. Do you feel you are enthusiastic and confident about your dream? If not what is stealing your enthusiasm and your confidence.

_____

_____

_____

_____

_____

5. Is your dream or project presented well to others so that they can receive it like you want them to?

_____

_____

_____

_____

_____

6. If your dream requires schooling have you taken the required courses in order to be an expert at your dream so that you can ensure your success if you're not already doing so? Why or why not?

_____

_____

_____

_____

_____

7. If not in what ways can you commit to completing the training needed to help you make your dream a success?

_____

_____

_____

_____

_____

8. If your dream requires network and marketing, do you feel like you are exploring all possible opportunities needed to pursue your dream? If yes in what ways have you done that? If no in what ways will you do this.

_____

_____

_____

_____

_____

9. Do you fill your consistent and disciplined enough to achieve your dream right now? If not what do you think is causing you to lack these things?

_____

_____

_____

_____

_____

10. Are you focused and do you have a realistic deadline in place? If so when and why do you feel this date is a substantial amount of time for you? If not what is stopping you from staying focused and putting a day in place?

_____

_____

_____

_____

_____

Chapter 9

1. Did you know that the power of your words concerning your dream can bring life or death to your ability to achieve it? In what ways are you mindful of your words?

_____

_____

_____

_____

_____

2. Understanding that whatever you put into the atmosphere vocally will eventually come back to you at the same frequency in which you sent it. Write down some positive words concerning your dream and your life's purpose and speak them out loud daily.

_____

_____

_____

_____

_____

3. Do you feel like prayer is the key to a successful dream coming to pass? Why or why not

_____

_____

_____

_____

_____

4. Do you pray over your dream? If you do what do you feel the Lord is saying, or what signs is He giving you concerning your dream.

_____

_____

_____

_____

_____

5. Without guilt or shame how often do you pray? If the answer is very little, what do you think is hindering you the most from talking to God?

_____

_____

_____

_____

_____

6. When you pray do you believe that your prayers will be answered? Why or why not?

_____

_____

_____

_____

_____

7. Do you believe that the Bible contains not only a roadmap to heaven but business principles that will help you along your journey? Why or why not?

_____

_____

_____

_____

_____

8. Are there any books besides the Bible that inspire you to pray and get closer to God? If so please describe and tell how that book changes your life.

_____

_____

_____

_____

_____

9. Are you willing to share this experience with someone else who is looking to find themselves as well as God? Explain how you will purposely help the next person along their journey.

_____

_____

_____

_____

_____

10. If there's any negative thoughts or words that come against your dream how will you counteract and cancel out this negativity.

_____

_____

_____

_____

_____

Chapter 10

1. Are you comfortable with connecting with others about your dream? why or why

   Not?

_____

_____

_____

_____

_____

2. Who was the first person that influenced you to pursue your dream and what was this person's relation and connection to you?

    _____

    _____

    _____

    _____

    _____

3. What type of connections do you feel are crucial for you in this season of your life?

    _____

    _____

    _____

    _____

    _____

4. Is there anyone that you feel you are supposed to be connected to for the sake of your dream? If so who is the person and why do you feel you're supposed to be connected to them?

    _____

    _____

    _____

_____

_____

5. Who are the 3 to 5 people already in your life right now that can help you to fulfill your dream?

_____

_____

_____

_____

_____

6. Is there currently anyone in your life that you feel has exhausted their time or overstayed their welcome? If so name them.

_____

_____

_____

_____

_____

7. Do you feel like people have a desire to connect with you concerning your dream? Why or why not

_____

_____

_____

_____

_____

8. Do you feel your dream matches your personality? Why or why not?

_____

_____

_____

_____

_____

9. On a scale of 1-10 how hot is the flame within your heart for your dream. (Circle one) 1 2 3 4 5 6 7 8 9 Explain the reason for your number.

_____

_____

_____

_____

_____

10. Are you living someone else's dream for your life? If so explain how you plan to start fulfilling your own dream.

_____

_____

_____

_____

_____

11. If your dream consist of you being in the public eye are you prepared for the attacks that will come? If so how have you prepared yourself?

_____

_____

_____

_____

_____

Chapter 11

1. Your dream cloud is the place where your dreams have come to pass and you are enjoying the fruits of your labor. Name a few dreams that have come to pass in your life?

_____

_____

_____

_____

_____

2. Do you feel like you have reached your dream cloud? Why or why not?

_____

_____

_____

_____

3. Understanding that Only God knows timing, how long before you see yourself living the dream life?

_____

_____

_____

_____

_____

4. How do you feel you achieving your goals and being on your dream cloud will benefit yourself and those around you?

_____

_____

_____

_____

5. Name your dream team, people that are committed to helping you achieve your dream no matter what it cost them.

_____

_____

_____

_____

_____

6.   If you are already on your dream cloud, do you feel you have burned some bridges? If so who and will you humble yourself enough to make it right?

_____

_____

_____

_____

_____

7.   In what ways are you careful about the mate that you select to go on this dream journey with you?

_____

_____

_____

_____

_____

8.   Sometimes when our loved ones see the change in our lives they interpret this success as conceit. Do you have people in your life that think you have forgotten about them? If so how do you deal with this? If this hasn't happened to you, how would you handle it if this was your case?

_____

_____

_____

_____

_____

9. Would you say you are humble enough to be successful and to live on your dream cloud? Why or why not?

_____

_____

_____

_____

_____

10. As God increases your life can you commit to genuinely giving him glory and honor for every success no matter large or small? If so write down some of the ways you will do this.

Index of scripture

Chapter 1

Proverbs 3:6 says "in all your ways acknowledge Him, and He shall direct your path."

James 2:17 says "thus also faith by itself, if it does not have works, is dead."

Genesis 2:19-20 "out of the ground the Lord God formed every beast of the field and every bird of the air, and brought them to Adam to see what he would call them. And whatever Adam called each living creature that was its name, so Adam gave names to all the cattle, to the birds of the air, and to every beast of the field."

Chapter 2

Jeremiah 1:5 "Before I formed you in the womb I knew you, before you were born I set you apart; I appointed you as a prophet to the nations."

Galatians 5:17 "For the flesh lusts against the Spirit, and the spirit against the flesh:

these are contrary to the other: so that you cannot do the things that you wish.

Matthew 26:40 – 41 "Then He came to the disciples and found them sleeping, and said to Peter, 'what! Could you not watch with me one hour? Watch and pray, lest you enter into temptation. The spirit indeed is willing but the flesh is weak.'"

Chapter 3

2nd Tim 1:7 "For God has not given us the spirit of fear; but of power, and of love, and of a sound mind."

Ecclesiastes 12:13. "Let us hear the conclusion of the whole matter: Fear God and keep His commandment, for this is the duty of all mankind."

Psalm 34:7 "The angel of the Lord encamps around those who fear Him, and delivers them."

Romans 2:11. "For there is no partiality with God"

Genesis 32:7

Psalms 27:1 "The Lord is my light and my salvation of whom shall I fear? The Lord is the strength of my life; of whom shall I be afraid?"

Chapter 4

Ecclesiastics 3:1 "To everything there is a season and a time to every purpose under heaven."

Galatians 6:9
"Let us not be weary in well doing: for in due season we shall reap if we faint not."

First John 1:9 says "if we confess our sins God is faithful and just to forgive us our sin and to cleanse us of all unrighteousness."

Chapter 5

Genesis 3:7-10 says "The eyes of both of them were opened, and they knew that they were naked; and they sewed fig leaves together and made themselves coverings. And they heard the sound of the Lord God walking in the garden in the cool of the day so Adam and his wife hid themselves from the presence of the Lord God among the trees of the garden. The Lord God called to Adam and said to him where are you? So he said I heard your voice in the garden and I was afraid because I was naked so I hid."

Luke 15:11

John 15:18 Jesus said "if the world hates you, you know that it hated me before it hated you."

1 John1:9 "if we confess our sins, he is faithful and just to forgive us our sins and to cleanse us from all unrighteousness."

Judges 7:13-14

Genesis 12:12 – 13 "Therefore it will happen, when the Egyptian see you, that they will say, this is his wife; and they will kill me, but they will let you live. Please say you are my sister that it may be well with you for your sake, and that I may live because of you."

John 11:25, 16 "Jesus said unto her I am the resurrection and the life: and he that believes in me, though he may die, yet shall he live: and whosoever live and believes in me shall never die."

Hebrews 9:27 says "and as it is appointed for man to die once, but after this comes judgment."

Philippians 1:21 "For me to live is Christ and to die is gain"

Chapter 6

Hebrews 11:6 "that without faith it is impossible to please him, for he who comes to God must believe that He is a rewarder of those that diligently seek Him."

Matthew 17:20 "Because of your unbelief, for assuredly, if you have faith as a mustard seed, you will say to this mountain, move from here to there, and it will move; and nothing will be impossible for you."

John 2:3

Chapter 7

Malachi 3:16 – 18 says "then thou who fear the Lord spoke to one another, and the Lord listened and heard them so a book of remembrance was written before him for those who fear the Lord and who meditate on his name. They shall be mine, says the Lord of hosts, on the day that I make them my jewel. I will spare them as a man spares his own son who serves him. Then you will again discern between the righteous and the wicked, between one who serve God and one who does not serve God."

Matthew 7:22 – 23 Jesus says "many will say to me in that day, Lord, Lord, have we not prophesied in your name, cast out demons in your name, and done many wonders in your name? And then I will declare to them, I never knew you: depart from me, you who practice wickedness."

Chapter 8

Habakkuk 2:2 tells us "right the vision and make it plain on tablets."

Chapter 9

Proverbs 18:21 reminds us that "Life and Death are in the power of the tongue and those who love it will eat its fruits."

Galatians 6:7 says "Do not be deceived; God is not mocked: for whatever a man sews, that he will also reap."

Isaiah 55:11 says "so shall my word be that goes forth from my mouth; it shall not return to me void, but it shall accomplish that which I sent it, and it shall prosper in the thing which I sent it."

Mark 11:24 tells us "Therefore I say to you, whatsoever things you asks when you pray, believe that you receive them, and you will have them."

Hebrews 11:6. "Without faith it is impossible to please God"

2nd Corinthians 5:7. "We walk by faith and not by sight"

Chapter 11

Matthew 23:12 and said "and who ever exalts himself will be humbled, and he who humbles himself will be exalted."

Hebrews 12:11 "no discipline seems pleasant at the time, but painful. Later on, however, it produces a harvest of righteousness for those who have been trained by it."

Matthew 6:26 says "look at the birds of the air; they do not so or read, neither do they reap, nor do they gather in their barn, and yet your heavenly father feeds them. Are you not worth much more than they?"

Acknowledgments

I thank God first and foremost for giving me a second chance at life. There was a time when I didn't want to go on, a time when I didn't see a future for myself, but God showed me a light that I could not resist. His love and compassion towards me has given me the confidence to walk in grace, having no fear of the opinions of others. I also want to acknowledge my mother Evette for continually being a reflection of love. To my grandmother Ann, and my aunt Mae for raising me to be a woman of integrity. A special thanks to Mr. Larry and Mrs. Lola, who adopted me as an addition to their family at the start of my adulthood. To the man of God over my life prophet Theodore from call to holiness international ministries for continually speaking life into me and believing in my purpose. I want to acknowledge my cousin Aquarius who was one person that I sought wisdom from. I appreciate my mentor Shelly Martin for her input and direction on my approach to this platform.

To my brothers La'Quan and Kyree, for sharing their wisdom and advice. I want to thank my sister Domilola I appreciate her help with multiple revisions. When my spirit was down and times felt rough I would lean on my best friend Lisa. I want to thank my friend Tatiana for all of the text messages and phone calls that inspired me to keep going. To Troy my lifelong friend for his continued encouragement and support. A special thanks to my aunt Anekia for being a backbone to me and being there throughout the years. To my aunt Latrice who always who influenced me even as a little girl with her positive words. Thanks to my cousins Whitlee and Mersayteis for being there for me like my sisters. I want to acknowledge Minister Teasha for training me to be a true servant to the body of Christ. I also appreciate my friend Stacy for her support and dedication on this project with me. I want to give an honorable thanks to Drs. David and Tracy Forbes for grooming me to be on fire for Jesus and laying the foundation. I am most appreciative to Laura for spending countless hours editing this book. I'm extremely grateful for Vincent and max for designing the cover and making it a success. And may God bless everyone who believed in this dream; I pray that this message is a blessing to you like it was to me. And remember your first audience is yourself.

Reference page

(Hinn, 1990)

Printed in the United States
By Bookmasters